Comfort for Hard Times

Also by Louis Bauer

Alpha and Omega, Vol. I

Alpha and Omega, Vol. II

Archie the Archangel (a children's book)

Also by Susan Bauer

Choosing Africa

Comfort for Hard Times

*Meditations on Solace,
Hope, and Healing*

Louis E. Bauer

———————

Hawfields Press
Mebane, North Carolina

ISBN 978-1-60145-748-6

Hawfields Press
Mebane, North Carolina
2018

Printed in the United States of America on acid-free paper

First Edition

Cover illustration by Susan Bauer

For Jason and Megan

Contents

Editor's Preface

My husband Lou was a man of The Word and a man of words. He was a Lutheran pastor who served five congregations throughout his forty-nine years of ministry. Lou and I also served as missionaries in Africa for six years, where we taught seminarians in Namibia and Ghana. At one of these seminaries, Lou was also the Dean of Students.

Lou's post-graduate training in counseling and his care for deeply troubled people, many of whom lived in psychiatric facilities, made him acutely aware of the often unspoken suffering and troubledness of the persons entrusted to his care in those churches and seminaries. As a priest and preacher, Lou endeavored to bring God's Good News to the person in the pew. Lou was awed by the mystery of this God of ours who could create quarks and cosmos, while caring so tenderly for each of us. Someone recently asked me what I thought was the most distinguishing feature of my husband's preaching, and I immediately replied, "He sought to bring comfort."

When Lou died in September 2016, he left behind a stack of unpublished sermons. Many of his more recent sermons had been published as meditations in his two previous books, *Alpha and Omega: Meditations on the Divine Mystery, Volumes I and II*. It was my great privilege to edit those books, transforming—with his guidance and approval—sermons into personal meditations for the reader. After his death, as I read through the many sermons he had left, I realized how powerfully the theme of comfort resounded throughout his writing. Even in my own deepest moments of grief, I felt embraced by those words of God's grace. I knew that I wanted—needed—to share those comforting words with others who were hurting. I have gently edited them for the reader.

Another gift I received during my first year of bereavement was the discovery of blessings, specifically in Jan Richardson's book, *The Cure for Sorrow: A Book of Blessings for Times of Grief* and John O'Donohue's *To Bless the Space Between Us: A Book of Blessings*. O'Donohue tells us: "(Blessing) is not the invention of what is not there, nor the glazed-eyed belief that the innocent energy of goodwill can alter what is destructive. Blessing is a more robust and grounded presence; it issues forth from the confident depth of the hidden self, and its vision and force can transform what is deadlocked, numbed, and inevitable. When you bless someone, you literally call the force of their infinite self into action." (p.207)

I humbly offer the reader short blessings following each of my husband's meditations. Unless otherwise indicated, all of the blessings are my creation.

May you find hope and comfort here.

Susan Bauer 2018

Introduction

*That evening they brought to him
many who were possessed with
demons; and he cast out the spirits
with a word, and healed all who were
sick. This was to fulfill what was
spoken by, the prophet Isaiah, "He
took our sickness and bore our pain."*
(Matthew 8: 16-17)

*I*t was evening. The sun was setting, and it was
the cool and calm time of the day. Matthew
paints a picture for us. There are crowds—large
crowds—inching their way toward the Rabbi,
reaching out to him. There is a solidarity of
experience in these people who are pressing
forward. They know something of life's
brokenness. Either they are diseased or someone
they know and love is ill. Everyone in that
crowd pressing toward Jesus that evening had
come to him profoundly aware of their need to
be healed. What distinguishes this crowd of sick
and ailing humanity is just that: they are aware
of their need.

This evening's round of healings was the climax to a busy day for Jesus. Matthew reminds us that on that same day a leper had come to Jesus and said, "If you will, you can make me clean." A centurion had come to him on behalf of his paralyzed servant said to him, "Just say the word, and my servant will be healed."

You begin to perceive this powerful, image of people coming to Jesus. They are bringing him their aches and pains, their sorrows and transgressions, their disappointment and their grief. Some are paralyzed. Some are fevered. Some are disabled. Some are depressed. Some are simply wounded by life. But they come, knowing their need. And they come trusting that he can do something for them, believing that he can heal them.

And that is the point, isn't it? Especially if what is ailing us may not be readily apparent to our family and our friends. We are first invited to recognize our need for healing, because no healing is possible unless we first have the courage to acknowledge our need to be restored and renewed. We are invited to come to this gentle healer with the same kind of trust displayed by those brave souls we encounter in Matthew's Gospel. This implicit trust means that if we dare to lay our infirmity, our weakness, our illness, and our pain upon Jesus, we can experience healing. We can experience wholeness.

I encourage you to quietly ponder your own neediness, and I encourage you to dare to bring it to God for healing, trusting that he desires and wills your wholeness. You will soon realize that you are not alone. You will soon know that you have already moved beyond weakness and infirmity to strength and love. We come to God, imploring, "Take our infirmities and bear our diseases." Remember the leper who called out, "If you will, you can make me clean." In the ultimate act of love, Jesus replies to each of us who come to him just as he replied to the leper: "I will."

Lou Bauer

Peter's Journey

Let me offer the following short passage, from the Book of Acts, for you to tuck into the back of your mind as you read this meditation:

The members of the Council were amazed to see how bold Peter and John were and to learn that they were ordinary men of no education...They realized then that they had been companions of Jesus.

I invite you to ponder with me what it means to engage upon a spiritual journey. Now by "spiritual journey" I do not mean a trek down the aisle to a pew. I do not mean a pilgrimage to the Holy Land or the Vatican. I don't think I even mean reading a number of religious or devotional books. All of these things may be helpful, but, really, I don't think a spiritual journey has anything to do with what goes on out in the world.

The movement of a spiritual journey is inward, plunging deep into the inner recesses of yourself. Those who embark upon a spiritual journey are going somewhere. They are searching for something in their quest. They are yearning. The people I have known who have launched forth on a spiritual journey have realized that there is nothing in this life that seems to satisfy their nagging, restless hunger. Those on a spiritual journey are empty and seeking to be filled. They have come to know that there is nothing in this world that they have tried that can satisfy their hunger. Not financial security. Not sex. Not intellectual challenge. Not even another person, as dear as that person may be. And, surprisingly, not even religion!

Spiritual journeys are not for everyone. Like all journeys, they are fraught with dangers. But they offer the potential for an encounter with the sublime. With God. Most people, however, will live out their lives never having left home on a spiritual journey. Sadly, they will have missed out on what might be the only reason for life itself.

Would you like to leave where you are right now and embark upon a spiritual journey? You will travel into what will seem like a strange, sometimes frightening, yet sweet place. Are you a member of a church? A church itself is not the journey, but the church can offer you sustenance along the way: a piece of bread, a cup of wine, some words of promise, and water to cleanse and refresh. What will you need to bring? You will have to provide yourself: all your experiences, all your hurts, all your sorrows, all your joys, and all your victories. You will have to provide the good parts and the bad parts of yourself, what you cherish and what you despise about yourself.

You will also need an ear tuned to silence. An ear that can hear through the silence of unanswered prayer. An ear to listen for the voice of the Holy One speaking your name.

A fisherman sat by the lake, mending his nets and preparing his fish for delivery. He sat there pondering his life, his wife and children, and his cantankerous mother-in-law. His life was like those nets: in need of mending and full of holes through which the best catch always slipped away. He had enough perhaps to survive, but, like the nets, he was often empty. He was hungry. Not for another mackerel, but for food to feed his soul.

Then one day, as he tried again to patch all the holes in his nets, a voice said to him, "Follow me." And he left his nets, still in need of mending, and journeyed along after this incredible voice. He was a fool. Everyone thought so. But he had found a path down which to travel. A journey had begun. And he pursued that voice as the voice called the dead back to life and exorcised the demons who possessed the common folk. As the voice spoke so tenderly to the little folk, to those who had been forgotten by life, and also to the big folk who had forgotten what life was. The voice freed people of their guilt. Lifted the fallen and depressed. Breathed a new spirit into life. And it was a powerful spirit that announced that life was, and could be, good and rich for anyone who was daring or desperate enough to engage in the journey and follow him.

This man, Peter, was not very bright. It wasn't the first time he had been called an "ordinary man." Fishermen didn't attend the great schools. He couldn't even sign his own name. But, you see, you don't have to be anyone other than an ordinary person to find yourself on a spiritual journey. In fact, the more intelligent you are, the more difficult the journey seems to be. Not impossible, just more difficult.

For the first time, the man found life to be sweet. There was something breathtaking every day…which made it easier to bear the hunger, to sleep in caves, and to get pushed around by crowds of people who also wanted to hear the voice. Then one day, partway through his journey, the voice turned to him and stunned the man with a question. Now the man had already been thinking about this question, but he did not have an answer ready. Again the voice inquired, "Who do you think I am?"

The man searched his soul for some kind of answer that would not disappoint his companion, the one who had shown him a new way to live, a way free of burdens. Then, from deep within, he heard the words forming and he heard himself speaking with his own words, but propelled by another force, "You are the Christ, the Son of the living God."

No one ever finds that answer within herself or himself. It is given to those who take the journey and follow him. It is a gift. And, as the elders at the council wisely perceived, Peter's boldness and insight came by the only way it ever comes on the spiritual journey: by becoming a companion with Christ. Or, in words that often embarrass the sophisticated, by walking with Jesus.

And the voice replied, "You are Peter, and on this rock I will build my church." This church is nothing more than a band of seekers. Many of us are wounded in various ways, but Christ's precious gift of himself steadies us as we journey through life to encounter the God of life. Are you ready to be as brave and as ordinary as Peter, to begin your spiritual journey?

~~~

When the whisper of the Spirit
stirs a current of sweet longing and hope
within your own ordinary life,
may you have the courage
to step out and into the journey
where the voice of the Holy One speaks your name.

When Bad Things Happen

*I*n 1981 Rabbi Harold Kushner wrote a book that shot to the top of the best seller list. Perhaps you have read this popular book, *When Bad Things Happen to Good People*. Rabbi Kushner's book was his effort to struggle with a deeply personal question: why is there evil in the world? He knew the reality of evil in his own life. He had experienced anguish in the death of his son Aaron. So he wrote his book in an attempt to account for the suffering that so many of us experience in life. The popularity of the book had far more to do with the question he raised than with the answer he gave.

Kushner touched upon a reality that brings many to the realms of the religious in search of an answer to this most difficult of questions. Why is there evil? Why must we suffer? My many years as a pastor, as well as my own personal experiences, have convinced me that this is one of the fundamental reasons why people cross the threshold of churches. We come, primarily, because we have known the effects of evil and of suffering. We are searching for the triumph of goodness. Our search is for a foundation of hope upon which we may build our lives.

Jesus encountered many people who asked Rabbi Kushner's question. As so often happens to any healer—whether he is a physician or she is a psychologist or a pastor—Jesus was inundated. He was overwhelmed with people asking the question: Why do bad things happen to good people, such as ourselves? Perhaps you have also asked that same question. Perhaps you are asking it today.

How does Jesus respond to this most painful human question? He responds in the way he favors most. He thinks that we can best understand life and reality in stories. So he tells a story about a man who sowed seed.

A man went out to sow good seed. From the very beginning of the story, we know that the seed sown is *good*. God's intention is good. What he has created is good. From the beginning God wills good for you and me. In spite of some of the dreadful conclusions we may reach about ourselves, *God has sown us as good seed*.

Then the parable says, "While everyone was sleeping..." I prefer to read that, "While you and I were not paying attention," an enemy came and sowed weeds among the good seed. Jesus has no name for what it is that opposes the goodness of God in life. All he says is that there is, indeed, a reality that works against the goodness and the fullness of life. Jesus expounds no great doctrine of evil. Rather, he simply and directly acknowledges that there is suffering. There is evil. There is that which works against the divine and his purposes.

The servants notice what has happened, and they come to the owner and ask, "What shall we do? Do you want us to pull up these weeds? Clear out all the evil? Root out everything that opposes and frustrates the purposes of God and the goodness of life?"

I pull weeds constantly. I pull them in my lawn. I pull them in our flower garden. I pull them in the churchyard. I tug and pull at the weeds that grow in the lives of my family and my parishioners.

Not so with the owner of the field who makes an astounding response. "Be careful, lest in pulling up the weeds, you destroy the good that I have done." The owner is willing to be patient, to bear with things. He is willing to suffer, confident that, at the appointed time, a rich harvest will follow. And so he commands his servants (you and I) to be patient and to bear with what seems to be broken in our lives and in the world.

Do not mistake this patience for indifference. It is patience borne of the deepest trust, the deepest surrender, that a good harvest will come. It is trust that the owner of the field who sowed the seed is in charge. *He* will distinguish between what is good and what is bad. *He* will gather the good, the fruit of what he has sown, into his barns.

What Jesus teaches here is that you and I have to live with ambiguity in this life. But in living with ambiguity, we can remain confident that everything that is growing, everything that is struggling to give birth to the new, and everything that is on the side of growth and development will, in *his* time, reach fruition.

There has been no greater shortcoming in the Christian Church in recent years—actually, in recent centuries—than its failure to articulate and provide real hope for the fullness of life beyond the here-and-now. To proclaim the eternal harvest that awaits us. If you do not grasp that hope, the constant hope of the Christian future, then you are, as St. Paul says, "the most miserable of all people."

The story of the sower is one of Jesus's most optimistic and exciting parables. The sower is in charge. He sows good seed. He waits. He knows there will be resistance, but that doesn't destroy him or devastate him. He commands his servants to be patient, to wait in confidence. And then he orders his harvest to be gathered into his barns.

We are not called to save ourselves. Or the world. In fact, our many proposals to do so are often fraught with great danger. We would mess up the crop in the process. It is enough for us to trust that God has our lives and his world surrounded by the arms of the cross. Ultimately, the harvest will clarify and offer far more than you and I could ever imagine.

~~~

When the weight of despair
threatens to engulf you,
and the light of your life
has been snuffed out,
may a thin beam of hope
illumine your way
into the joy
that waits patiently for you.

When in Doubt

The day that we call Easter, three days after Jesus's crucifixion, was a heady day. The Lord finds it important to make sure his friends know what has happened. That he has, indeed, been raised from death. That he is alive!

In the morning, when the women who had followed him from Galilee go to his tomb with spices to anoint his body, they are astonished to learn that he is not there. In another telling of the story, Jesus appears to Mary Magdalene, who initially believes him to be the gardener. In the evening, Jesus appears to two of his friends, while they are walking on the seven-mile road from Jerusalem to the village of Emmaus. And that night, when the disciples are gathered together behind a locked door, fearful of what might happen to them, Jesus appears to the group and says, "Peace be with you."

But one of the disciples is missing. Where is Thomas? The Bible doesn't tell us. Perhaps he is so distressed, so overwhelmed by the death of his friend and his Lord, that he needs some time alone. When we grieve, some of us are comforted by the support of others who share our mourning. Others need solitude to absorb and ponder what has happened and what it means.

Thomas is astonished when his friends come to him with news that is either the cruelest joke or the most awesome fantasy: "We have seen Jesus!" But Thomas is not about to give his heart to cruel jokes or awesome fantasies. He has been disappointed—devastated—once. His world has fallen apart because he dared to trust. No, he will not allow himself to be that vulnerable again. He simply cannot believe what he hears.

So Thomas turns to his friends and says, "Unless I see in his hands the print of the nails, and place my finger in the mark of the nails, and place my hand in his side, I will not believe." And because Thomas dares to say this, something we would all like to say, he has come to be known as Doubting Thomas. The skeptic. But perhaps Thomas has been labeled a bit unfairly, simply because he cannot believe, at face value, what he hears.

There is something very subtle in what seems to be a rather brash and quarrelsome Easter story. You notice that Thomas does not say, "Unless I see the Lord, I will not believe." What clutched Thomas's heart was something deeper than seeing a ghost or an apparition or a vision. Thomas raises the compelling question of *identity*. I want to know that this *is* Jesus of Nazareth: the one in whom I trusted, the one I loved, the one who made my heart skip beats, the one who made life thrilling and rich.

What Thomas is really asking, what he is really wrestling with, is a question that many of us ask: What happens to us after death? What happens to those we love? Will they be recognizable?

Thomas does not doubt, as such, what he has been hearing. The number of witnesses is accumulating. They seem to have seen something. But there are also lots of ghosts flitting about Palestine, as well as rumors of other resurrections.

What stands before Thomas on this fateful evening in the upper room, and stands before us in this gospel story of Easter, is the need for an answer to the question: *Will our identities survive death intact?*

His hands open, and there before their eyes are the prints of the nails. He opens his garment to reveal the wound in his side. Yes, standing before Thomas is the wildest dream he can imagine, come true. Life does matter. History does matter.

The God who created us, the God who made us, the God who named us in our baptism, the God who has walked with us throughout life—although we have not always turned to him—has now completed creation. What he has begun in our mother's womb, he has brought to completion. Our lives do matter, because these moments and days are the beginning of eternity.

Now someone is going to ask a hard question. It is already forming in your heart: Why the wounds of Jesus? Are we not told that all things will be made new? Isn't there something incomplete here in this appearance before Thomas? Can we live with a wounded Jesus?

It is a tough question. But isn't this just as it must be? Isn't this the way of the God who is willing to take the woundedness of suffering and death and transform it into triumph? Isn't the strength of Jesus in his wounds?

Perhaps this revelation of woundedness also points us to a new dimension of the power and beauty of the Easter reality. Each of us has been wounded in one way or another. Each of us has felt the pain of life. Each of us knows life's deep and hurtful realities. Perhaps some of us would want to do away with our wounds, transform the scars on our hearts. But to change all that is to change who we are. To change all that would be to obliterate our identities and to dismiss as irrelevant all that our life is. The Easter story for Thomas is that God takes life, in all its wounded brokenness, and transforms it into something new. Our wounds are healed, but the scars remain. Our hurt is assuaged, and we are who we are. The moments and days spent together in friendship and love flow into eternity, and we will know one another.

I wonder what Thomas said to himself as he left the upper room that night, as he walked down the road to his home, while everyone else dozed in the calm of renewing sleep. I suspect you might have heard him whispering through the streets of Jerusalem: We shall survive for he is risen.

If you search with your heart, if you listen with all your being and imagination, if you live, not from vacation to vacation, but from the divine miracle of one precious moment of your life to the next precious moment, what you may see and hear is the resurrected Lord himself.

What you may hear is the gentle voice of the Lord somewhere deep within you, reminding you that your life has a divine purpose, whether you can understand it or not. This holy purpose embraces you, through all your doubting, faithlessness, and fear until the moment when you suddenly know for sure that *everything makes sense*—divine sense—because everything that you are is in the hands of a loving God. Your life, your destiny, your death are all bound to him. And that, my friend, calls for real rejoicing.

~~~

When you dare to ponder
the end of your life
in this place we call home,
may you be suffused with the assurance
that the one who has known you from your birth
will bear you safely
into his eternal home,
scars and all.

Seeds of Comfort

*T*he parable Jesus tells about the sower and the seeds informs us that the seeds that fell on good soil "produced a crop—a hundred, sixty or thirty times what was sown."

In the liturgical year, this parable is frequently the gospel lesson for what I call Tomato Season. When I was a parish pastor, it was the time of year when many good and generous parishioners shared with my family the fruits of their tomato plants. If you were to come into our kitchen, you would have seen oodles of tomatoes arrayed upon the kitchen counters, a few unfortunate ones on the floor, and a big pot of tomato soup warming on the stove. So when Jesus speaks of the harvest being a hundredfold for the seed that fell upon good soil, I know personally how big that harvest can be. But this story is not about a harvest of tomatoes, but of grain.

Jesus, pressed in on all sides by the crowds at the lakeside, climbed into a boat to deliver a message of comfort and hope. His was a message of the deepest, profoundest optimism about life, told in a brief and simple story. Jesus, in his deep love for people, had a very specific reason for telling this little story. He wanted it to touch the hearts of these twelve people who had left their livelihoods to be God's servants. Jesus noticed that his twelve companions were becoming disillusioned and disappointed. His ministry was encountering resistance. The scribes and Pharisees were beginning to plot against Jesus. The occupying forces of Rome were becoming uncomfortable with his claims of another kingdom of ultimate power. It was beginning to dawn upon the twelve that all this talk about a cross might come true. Even for them! Life seemed to promise anything but fruitfulness and rich harvest.

But Jesus also told this little story of hope and comfort and profound optimism to the crowds. You see, he knew that someday there would be other crowds gathered, just as today, who would need the encouragement in life that comes from divine comfort.

He tells this story for the parents in the crowd who are disappointed in how their children were turning out. He tells this story for those who are reaching the autumn and winter years of their lives, with many of their dreams withering on the vine, their life feeling unfulfilled and unfruitful. He tells this story to the humble ones in the crowd, to remind them that the true warriors in the Kingdom of God are farmers, not soldiers. Farmers who sow seeds of peace and reconciliation, because God's kingdom comes not by revolution, but by the confident sowing of seeds of love. He tells this story for those in the crowd who have been disappointed in love and marriage. For those cloaked in grief. For those betrayed by family. For those oppressed by others more powerful.

Jesus tells this story for everyone in the crowd who mistakenly thinks that life can be evaluated before it is complete. Jesus tells this story for any who would dare to believe that life—each and every life—is a mystery held tenderly in the loving hands of God.

A sower went out to sow some seed. He tossed it here and he tossed it there. He is a person willing to risk, willing to live with a certain degree of abandon. He does not calculate or manipulate the seeds or tiny plants. Life—true life—can never be controlled or manipulated. Three-fourths of what he sows fails. Seventy-five percent failure is not a great statistic. Only a person with deep trust in the harvest would dare to set out in life against such formidable odds. But some of the seed takes to good soil and bears a rich harvest. And here is the real shocker: at best—the absolute, outside best—one could expect a ten-fold harvest of the seed sown. Anything beyond that is biologically impossible. But in Jesus's story, the harvest yields the staggering amount of one-hundredfold, sixtyfold, and thirtyfold. The harvest that God brings to life, according to Jesus, is beyond the most daring and wild imagination.

And because of that, one can dare to live life in profound hope, and profound optimism in the face of much disappointment.

You and I are called to be the sowers of seeds. It isn't our job to climb under the soil and push the plants up to fruitfulness. We can become confused and get that backwards in our lives. We are not responsible for the harvest. We are not called to try to save the world or other people or even ourselves. If we try to shoulder that heavy responsibility, we betray an ultimate disbelief in the salvation God wrought Friday afternoon on a cross in Jerusalem. We sow seeds, and then we trust in the spirit of God, in its own mysterious way and by its own mysterious schedule, to even bring life out of death in a shockingly one-hundredfold way.

I recall a conversation I once had with the mother of a young man I had confirmed about ten years earlier. He was one of my favorites: an extremely bright young boy who loved to discuss and debate what he was learning in his confirmation classes. He was the acolyte I could always depend on who would show up early to see if he were needed that morning. He was a crucifer who carried the processional cross with dignity, but with deep humility. But after he was confirmed, he turned cynical toward the church and religion. I seldom saw him anymore. At best, on Christmas Eve and Easter. A sown seed had died in the soil. Or had it been cast onto a stone or thistle?

A young medical intern was serving in the emergency room of a Philadelphia hospital. He called his mother and asked, "What is Pastor Bauer's phone number?" His mother asked him what he wanted with that phone number. He replied, "I want him to help me understand how to minister with these people here in their grief."

And there it was. The mystery of God and the one-hundredfold harvest.

Jesus told a brief story. A story of comfort. A story of hope for a world preciously short on hopefulness. A story of divine optimism. Linger with this story. He told it for your sake. Ponder it, discuss it, share it with someone. Sow a seed and be comforted, strengthened, and confident that although you may not reap what you sow, God is preparing for you an abundant harvest beyond your deepest dreams.

~~~

If you are the dutiful one,
exhausted from pushing up the grain,
fretting over the tender shoots,
this blessing arrives with a cup of cool water,
a soft shawl,
and an invitation to rest.
The harvest is assured.

You Are Not Alone

*J*esus peered deeply into their eyes, so deeply that he could see into their hearts, hearts saddened by the words he had just uttered: "I am leaving you." No one really likes to say goodbye. Saying farewell always hurts when you are leaving those whom you have deeply loved, those who have depended upon you. Jesus's farewell message to his friends is one of the most touching passages in the Scriptures. So let's open our hearts — use our imagination a bit — and join this farewell gathering of Jesus and his friends.

Jesus is seated at the table, peering deeply into the hearts of his friends, while the table is cleared, save for a loaf of bread and a cup of wine. They are all remembering their three years of living together and living for one another. They possessed nothing, really, but the elusive love of God between them. And yet, their cups of life overflowed with the simple joys of caring, healing, talking to one another about the truth. The disciples remembered how good it was to sit at the feet of the Master, listening to his words that somehow cut through all of life's hatred and ugliness to reveal an eternal love that could forgive anything. He even had shown them a glimpse of life that could overcome the deepest dread of the grave.

For the first time in their lives, these friends had felt whole in his presence. For once, life was more than just scraping by, it was really worth living. For once, they weren't afraid, neither of death, nor themselves, nor one another. Possessing nothing, somehow they had everything. They had Jesus. They had God! And life was incredible.

`But now he was leaving, and as Jesus looked deeply into their hearts, he saw the old fears resurging, just as they so often surge in our hearts. So he suggested something to them— something you and I need to hear today. He basically said to them, in his most tender voice, "My friends, you cannot make it alone in the world. In life."

Jesus knew that everyone of them (and everyone of us) would nevertheless try to make it alone, and that we would hurt ourselves— even destroy ourselves—as well as others. We would rather not admit that we can't make it alone. We'd rather not admit that we are dependent, somehow incomplete and not whole. We would rather grasp and grab and clutch and consume and quarrel and kill. We would try almost anything to make it, to transcend what so often rules the human heart and causes us heartaches in life: our fear of death, Our fear of extinction.

There is no other way to explain the way human beings are willing to live, with our greed and disregard for others, than to acknowledge that we are scared to death of death. And what's worse is that we won't admit it. All of our addictions, our fractured and broken relationships, our willingness to tolerate poverty for any human being, all of our defenses and weapons are but masks and symptoms of fragile souls who are scared to death of death. We fragile souls have yet to discover that there is hope beyond this tattered life of ours. Hope in the living God. So we continue to struggle to make it on our own, come hell or high water, and usually both do, in one form or another.

But now Jesus is leaving. He is turning those poor souls (and us) loose to face the world. He has to turn them loose, as a parent must free a child, or no one would ever grow. He says to them, across the loaf of bread and the cup of wine, "I will not leave you as orphans, abandoned. I will ask the Father, and he will give you another comforter to be with you forever.

Some translations of the Bible use the word "counselor" here, but that isn't quite right. It sounds like a guidance counselor or a pastoral counselor. No, he will give you a *comforter*, the Spirit of Truth. This Spirit of Truth speaks the comforting and caring words of grace, of eternity, of shepherding the flock through life, bringing each member of the flock home to good pasture. The Spirit of Truth speaks of what is real: that our fears of death are swallowed up in the divine. Because he lives, we will live also.

This Spirit of Truth is an infusion of God's presence in your life that can best be felt, heard and experienced in community. When we discover this Holy Comforter who loves us through life—who is, indeed, God—then we realize that we are bound to one another in a unique fellowship of mutual caring and support. When we accept that we are truly infused with the grace of God, there is really little else that we need, for we have nothing to fear, not even death itself. We become lights in the darkened world. We become yeast that gives life to the loaf of the world. We ourselves become what Jesus asks the Father to give us: we become holy comforters. Then, the orphaned of the world — and there are many who are living their lives as virtual orphans — are loved and reunited with the Father of us all.

Can you open your life to the Holy Spirit, the Comforter?

~~~

When your tattered life
and your shattered heart
drive you into
the dank cave of despair,
may the sweetest breeze
arrive to freshen you.
May the Holy Comforter
abide with you.

Nobody Knows My Name

*H*as this ever happened to you? You walk into a crowded room, all abuzz with little cadres of people laughing and talking with one another. You scan the room, searching for a familiar face or a smile of recognition. And then you realize no one in the room knows you. You recognize no one in the sea of faces. Down in the pit of your stomach is the aching realization that you are all alone, utterly unknown. Your eyes keep scanning the room, hoping that some friendly soul will greet you. Acknowledge that you exist.

Many of us have had that experience. For me it has been not uncommon. You see, deep down I am a rather bashful person. I tend to be insecure. A wallflower! I know well what it feels like to be lonely and unknown in a group of people. The moment I just described for you seems to last an eternity, doesn't it? And nothing would be sweeter at such a time than for someone to speak your name.

If someone were to speak your name, suddenly you would be connected. Someone would know you, because there is a whole person behind your precious name. A deep history. When someone speaks your name, you have an identity. No longer do you feel that you're in the wrong place at the wrong time. The deep, painful loneliness in the center of your heart melts...when someone speaks your name.

Your name says that you belong to someone. You're part of a family, the child of a father and mother. Such can be the power of speaking someone's name. If you don't think a name is important, just stop and consider how many times during a day you speak or write someone's name. Or consider a life without a name, if you can even imagine such a thing. Can you think of any lonelier life than a life lived as a nameless individual? Somehow, a name is more than just a few words. It encapsulates the identity of a person. A name becomes enmeshed with a person's very being. Swiss physician Paul Tournier, in his little book, *The Naming of Persons*, suggests that the act of naming a person confers a "thou-ness" upon the person. There seems to be something almost holy about the conferring of a name.

So why all this consideration of names? It is a way of peeling back layers of our social defenses so we can peer into the heart. And what do we see at the center of the human heart? Deep within each one of us, even the most popular, well-known, or outgoing of us, is a deep pocket of loneliness. What is peculiar about this loneliness is that no human being can ever reach it or allay it. Those whom we might see as bombastic are probably the loneliest of all among us. St. Augustine touched upon this when he suggested that the heart is restless until it finds God. Only in the life of God is our deepest loneliness overcome.

In John 10:1-19, Jesus tells us that he is the Good Shepherd. He knows his flock. "He calls his own sheep *by name* and leads them out." Can you believe it? God knows you by your name. There can surely be no deeper mystery than that God knows you amongst the vast cosmos and throng of humanity, living and dead. You are already named in eternity, never to be forgotten. Though you may feel nameless and faceless in a crowd, there is always One who knows you so intimately and cherishes you, that he beckons to your heart with your personal name. This is not the God of a crowd who yells out, "Hey, you!" No, with the deepest esteem and respect for you, he calls you by name.

Many of us live in transient communities. You make a friend, and just as you trust one another enough to really share your fragile selves with each other, one of you moves away. Or perhaps you have been betrayed by a friend. Or maybe someone precious to you has died. A natural reaction might be to close yourself up, like a turtle withdrawing into its protective shell, to make yourself immune to further pain. And who could blame you for wanting to avoid future hurt? But, you see, then you are right back to where you started—alone and lonely.

If the God who moves the planets and stars upon their paths knows you by your name, then can you risk being courageous enough to also reach out to another lonely soul? The greatest gift you can give another is to reach out with compassion, vulnerability, and true caring. When you can do this, you will know that God also sees that person and knows her or him by name and loves that person as a mother loves her child. When you share your humanity with another, you are also sharing God's divinity. You are no longer lonely strangers to one another on this journey of life, you are shepherds, called to care and speak the truth in love.

Then, together, we can even walk through the valley of the shadow of death, the final threat of loneliness, fearing no evil because the Good Shepherd is watching over us and bringing us home.

~~~

In the loneliness of the crowd,
when all you want to do
is to slip away,
this blessing is delighted to see you
and calls you by your name.

A Glimpse of the Unimaginable

Some years ago, J. B. Phillips, a well-known translator of the New Testament, wrote a little book entitled, *Your God is Too Small*. It was a simple little book that sought to respond to the trivializing of the divine, the reduction of God to an instrument to be manipulated to meet our needs. The title of his book stuck, and it is quoted frequently to those whose notion of the divine gets reduced down to what we can dream up from our experience.

There has always been, and will always be, those who would trivialize God. There will always be those whose comprehension of God is stunted and undernourished. These poor souls have a dwarfed perception of the Almighty.

So it was in an encounter between Jesus and a group of people called Sadducees. The Sadducees were a conservative sect that accepted only the written Law of Moses. We might see them as first century fundamentalists. They could find no solid reference in their scriptures for resurrection.

Modern Christians might be surprised that early Judaism had little concern for life after death. References to it in the Hebrew Bible are slim. So the Sadducees, who took things pretty literally, had grave doubts about resurrection as a part of God's plan for his world.

A group of these Sadducees, with their dwarfed minds and rather antagonistic spirits, came to heckle Jesus with an impossible question: Rabbi, answer this one: a man dies and has no children. The law says that his brother must take his wife and have children. (Because, you see, that was how a person lived on—in the memory and genes of the next generation. To die without children was to go into extinction.) The second brother dies, and still there were no children. Five more brothers take up their duty and marry the woman, and each dies without children. And now, the question is not, "What's going to happen to the poor fellow who died first?" No, the trick question is, "Whose wife will the woman be in heaven?" And what is the answer? Be careful. This is more challenging than you might think.

Before we hear Jesus's reply, let me tell you what happens every time I read this story, or every time I tell this story to a group of people.

This whole story touches something very deep inside my personhood. Frankly, I don't care whose wife this woman will be. What I care about is *what will my relationships be like in heaven*? I simply cannot imagine not relating profoundly again with those with whom I have shared life so deeply. And as a pastor, I have had to be able to respond to this deeper question, which is what I think was really going on here anyway between the Sadducees and Jesus. Namely, the deeply personal, poignant question from the human heart: What happens to our relationships after we die?

There are some whose deepest desire and dream in life is to see their spouse again. They are so happily, intimately bound to their spouse that they could not ever imagine their relationship ever ending. There are also some so unhappily married that they can't wait. And there are some who have little desire to encounter again their ex-spouse. And that's only the beginning. Suddenly, every relationship falls into this realm of questioning. Do we face again the relative to whom we never said good-bye? Or the one who damaged our lives? Or the one who abused us?

Are any of these questions even answerable? When Jesus replied to the Sadducees' question, his answer was so profound, Luke tells us, that he silenced his questioners and no one dared to take him on again.

His answer to their question, and to our questions, is brief and direct: our relationships are transfigured. They are perfected. Our identities are transformed into children of God. Everyone throughout time relates perfectly. And Jesus is willing to say nothing more. He has said enough. He has affirmed the resurrection and the transfiguration of every human relationship into a perfect communion.

Now, if we were to grasp the stunning depth of what Jesus has affirmed, what might that do to our broken relationships with others, particularly those closest to us? Might we not be a bit more patient, a bit more loving, a bit more forgiving? Might we become capable of seeing another person as one of God's creatures on the road with us, being transformed and transfigured into what God has chosen her or him to be?

Perhaps it will be easier when we realize that the "her or him" is you and me. Our relationships can be transfigured even here, even now, in response to our Lord's command to, "Love one another, as I have loved you."

"And whose wife will she be?" What a trivial question! What foolish thinking from dwarfed minds. Jesus will not engage in penetrating the impenetrable, except to lift the curtain for a brief glimpse into the unimaginable.

Here is an image that might allow us to glimpse the mystery that answers the questions we ask from our hearts. Perhaps we are like a fetus, gestating to full term, carried safely in a womb we cannot see, by a love we have not yet seen face-to-face. We swim in a vast darkness with no idea, and no way of even imagining from our experience, what awaits us outside the womb. We do not even know there is a world yet to come. But suddenly we find ourselves thrust into the light of day.

The difference between the infant waiting to be born and ourselves is that we are swimming about in this amniotic fluid of life. It's complicated. Sometimes downright scary. Often we will stumble. But we have heard the story of Christ's resurrection and his promise of relationships transfigured and yet to come. And

we live, trusting that promise we have heard.
We dare to risk loving others as he has loved us.
We have no other purpose, as people of God,
than to live boldly and joyfully this promise of
resurrection and transfiguration of all
relationships. It is worth the risk. It is
everything.

~~~

May God's gentle grace
heal what is broken in your life,
and may you, too, catch a glimpse
of the transformation that awaits you.

Come to the Table

Let's imagine ourselves at another time, and in another place. Strangely, it is a place we have all been, and perhaps a place where we still are. We are in a spacious room together. It is apparently a dining room, for there is a large table in the center of the room. The table is laden with food: bright oranges, healthy figs, clusters of grapes. Loaves of fresh bread, their yeasty aroma filling the air, are stacked high upon one end of the table. At the other end are platters of succulent roasted meats. Hmmm, this has all the makings of a genuine feast.

Over to the left of the room is a group of people. They are whispering and pointing. Their faces betray the intensity of these people. Over on the right side of the room is another group of people. These people are inching their way toward the table, to sit close to someone who is already seated there, sampling some of the delicacies.

What seems so strange, though, is that although there are two distinctly separate groups of people in this room, it is hard to find anything that really differentiates them from each other. They look very similar in appearance, their clothes are the same, they are about the same age, and no one is better groomed, or more poorly groomed, than anyone else. Yet somehow these people who are virtually the same have divided themselves into two different groups. Why? There is nothing we can see that should make them differ.

The people on the left are called Pharisees. They are teachers of God's law and are very bright. They have keen intellects and are devout in their convictions. And the other group? Those inching toward the table to sit with the guest of honor? Ah, they are tax collectors and sinners. People who have made mistakes in life. Do you see yourself in one of these groups yet? Which one—the group on the left or the group on the right?

But let's dispense with the labels of Pharisee, tax collector, and sinner, because labels aren't real. Let's, instead, look into their hearts. When we peer into the hearts of the ones on the left, the ones who are pointing, what we see is frightening. Their hearts are made of stone. When we turn to the people on the right, the ones inching ever closer to the table, we see that their hearts are broken. There is sadness, heaviness, grief, and pain surrounding these broken hearts.

They begin to look more familiar to us now. Some of us are in the group with them, tip-toeing toward a seat near the one who is sitting at the festive table. Some of these are simply lonely people who don't fit in anywhere. They have been excluded by life, and nothing could be sweeter to their ears than to hear someone say, *I care*, and mean it. Just to be accepted as they are. Oh, how they yearn to be loved.

Others have made mistakes—some of them big mistakes. They have already paid dearly for their failures. They don't need to be reminded or labeled. They already believe that there isn't much about them that's worth very much. No, they don't need to be judged. They just need to be loved.

Each one of them (each one of us?) already has a voice deep down inside that whispers doubt about their worth. They all have their inner punisher who berates them. They know that nothing could be sweeter than a love that could embrace them, lift them up. An infinite love, with no strings attached.

And so they — we — inch closer, to sit next to the man at his banquet table. Somehow they know that to be near him is to be in the presence of someone who accepts you as you are. He knows the pain in your broken heart before you even put it into words. He absorbs that pain into his body and he touches your trembling heart and heals it. He makes it beat again with new life.

To sit next to him is to sit in the presence of a love that cleanses and purifies, like no love anyone has ever known before. This love is so pure, so caring. Life in his presence is as good as it was always meant to be. Such love can heal any heart, forgive any sin, and accept any person. No one feels guilt in his presence, and his love makes you want to be a lover yourself.

The great medieval poet Dante, in his magnificent poem *The Divine Comedy*, described the God who was present in this young rabbi from Nazareth, as "the love which moved the stars and planets on their way." Love and compassion center the universe, and all of life is ruled by this compassionate God whose only purpose is to love unendingly.

This love that Dante so described is seated there at the table, waiting for us to come and dine with him. He won't send us away hungry because his favorite people are those who need him. They are the ones who hunger and thirst for acceptance. And Jesus actually enjoys being with the likes of you and me and all the others around us who inch near his table.

But let me tell you a secret about the Christ who sits at the table in the room. His heart aches, even for those who are pointing at you and me. He yearns for them to come and join him, that he might melt their frozen hearts with his grace. But they refuse to approach the table. They cannot take that step that the broken-hearted know they must take. The Pharisees could only approach him through his disciples.

And what about you? Are you inching toward him, willing to risk the ultimate to receive the ultimate, to give your heart to him?

~~~

All this blessing wants
is to take your hand
and bring you to your seat
at the table,
for the Lord
delights in your presence.

The Great Healer

I once served as the pastor of a congregation in Chapel Hill, North Carolina. Just blocks from the church was the University of North Carolina Medical Center, a sprawling complex of medical buildings offering state-of-the art medical care for any ailment. Seven miles away was Duke Hospital, another outstanding facility. In fact, when you travel the road from Chapel Hill to Durham, you will see a road sign: Durham — City of Medicine. Excellent health care is (along with basketball) one of the most significant identifying features of this area.

I recall once asking members of an adult Sunday school class to introduce themselves. I was amazed that more than half of them identified themselves as being associated with the healthcare profession. Yet, when I suggested to the congregation that we would hold a Service of Healing and Wholeness, eyebrows were raised. Faces assumed puzzled looks. What is he talking about? We are not terribly comfortable with the notion of a healing ministry in the church. That's something for physicians and hospitals, for scalpels and antibiotics. The mention of healing in the church conjures up images of crutches lining the grotto at Lourdes or of an evangelist seizing a paralyzed person by the head and shouting, "Heal!"

And yet, a significant portion of Jesus's ministry was healing those whose lives were broken. He sent forth his disciples on missions that included healing. One of the early followers of Jesus, and a close companion of St. Paul, was actually a practitioner of the healing arts, Saint Luke the physician. Luke wrote one of the most beautiful gospels about the life of Jesus. He also wrote the history of the earliest church in the Book of Acts. Luke is often referred to as "the beloved physician."

Luke the Physician saw that at the heart of the healing reality in life stands the figure of Jesus Christ. Here was a doctor who recognized that what heals each of us—our broken bodies, our fragmented souls, our ruptured relationships, our pains, our anxieties, our fears—can only be found in the profoundest miracle of all: the miracle of Jesus the Christ. Luke's testimony is that all miracles of healing, whether at the hands of a physician, a nurse, or a counselor, find their sources in the God who reaches out in love in Jesus Christ to heal us of what most deeply afflicts us and pains us in life.

If you read carefully the Gospel of Luke the Physician, you will discover that this great doctor clearly perceived the sickness for which we most need the healing touch. It is the fear of death. We recognize that we are finite, and our resulting anxiety to make something of our short lives on this Earth drives us into all kinds of brokenness. In an ironic twist, we seek to allay our anxiety by habits and addictions that are self-destructive, and we end up hurting those closest to us. We engage in wars because we are frightened. Frightened of our mortality. We are in bondage to sin, and we need healing. We need wholeness. We need the comfort of being touched by nothing less than the hand of God who has overcome death and promises the astounding reality of resurrection.

Listen to the physician and hear what he discovered to be the greatest healing miracle of all: the healing of all of your brokenness, your pain, and your sorrow has been overcome by the wounded Jesus who has been raised to life. And because he lives, we will also live with God eternally. Beyond our deepest fears and anxieties is a God so loving that he reaches out to assure us in person that we are his, and that nothing in this life can separate us from the life yet to come in Christ. *This* is the fundamental ministry of healing entrusted to his Church.

When I was the pastor of that congregation in Chapel Hill, I held a memorial service and scattered the ashes of a tiny infant born four months prematurely. Actually this infant was the second of twins, the first having spontaneously aborted. The father of the tiny infant was a resident at the medical center a few blocks away. When I went to see the young couple on the evening after their second infant had died, I shared in their sorrow as we made plans for the brief service. When I was about to leave their apartment, tears welled up in the eyes of the father, the young healer, and he said to me, "Pastor, I have one more question." Sobbing, his voice cracking, he asked, "Pastor, will I see my child again?" There was a moment of silence. He had asked the fundamental question of life's brokenness. The plea for ultimate healing had been uttered.

What would you have said to him? How would you have answered? I turned to him and replied, as Luke the Physician would have replied, "Yes, my friend, you will see your child again, for in Christ we shall all be transformed and raised to life again." And in that moment, God's great miracle in Christ brought healing, comfort, and wholeness to a shattered father. He nodded his head in agreement, and a small smile of joy broke through his veil of tears.

~~~

May the gentle touch
of the Wounded Healer
ease your affliction and fear
and restore you
to wholeness and life everlasting.

The Wisdom to Withdraw

The golden dawn had not yet broken in Capernaum when Jesus slipped outside the city. Perhaps he walked quietly in the darkness to the nearby Sea of Galilee. He needed a lonely place to rest his bruised self in solitude. The night's rest seemed little more than a catnap, hardly enough sleep to restore his aching body, his tense muscles, and his bruised soul. As he walked out of the city before the first rays of sunlight would rouse this suffering humanity, he reflected upon the previous grueling day. His ministry had just begun. Would it always be like this?

First, there was the teaching in the temple and its sudden interruption by a flailing demoniac. Then, on to Peter's house where he ministered to his fever-bound mother-in-law. And just as he was about to rest, when dusk had settled over Capernaum, the crowds had gathered at the door, pressing in upon him, laying at his feet all their broken dreams, their crippled children stunted by disease, their elders gnarled by old age. Pain and suffering engulfed the neighborhood and even threatened to suffocate Jesus.

There is a stench that every healer knows. It hovers over so much suffering humanity. It exhausts one—the endless lines of suffering that lead one to wonder if she or he has really healed anyone because the people just keep coming.

Jesus was weary. Drained. On the edge of burnout already, and his ministry was but a few days old. He had tossed and turned in bed that night and could not sleep. So, deep into the night, he decided to search for strength in the only way he knew how. He went off alone to pray.

Our Lord needed such a time to break away from life's intensity. He needed space and time to be alone with the very ground of his being. If Jesus knew how to satisfy these deepest needs, then why do we so often dare to live life with such uninterrupted intensity? Do we think we are in control of our destinies? Or do we believe that nothing could come from a quiet period of prayer? You might be surprised to discover, in reading the Gospel of Mark, how our Lord's life follows a rhythm of engagement with life and a period of withdrawal when he rests in God's graciousness. These are times of reflection and even redirection. Every time a major crisis looms in Jesus's life or before he embarks upon a task, we find him quiet and alone, listening in silence for the quiet voice of his Father. Jesus spent forty days alone in the desert before launching his encounter with life. He was alone in Gethsemane, praying his heart out, before the final few days of his life. And here he is now, outside the city of Capernaum, pondering the flood of experiences of the previous day.

Was his time alone with the Father simply a waste of time? Useless prayer? Time which could have been better spent in mastering life? Or is Jesus the quintessential example of one who reveals the ultimate mystery that time "wasted" with God is the mark of spiritual maturity?

Something happened that morning in the lonely place. We do not know what Jesus thought about, what he pondered, or what he might have prayed about. Mark doesn't tell us. But something decisive happened. No sooner has the sun begun to waken Capernaum, than the disciples are pursuing Jesus—and you hear the intensity in the word *pursuit*—because the whole town is searching for him and his power. Jesus is again at the edge of falling into that same trap of frantic, draining activity in which so many of us find ourselves enmeshed.

But something happened in that solitude with God. His reply to the disciples shows us that. A major correction of his life has emerged from his communion with God. "Let us go to the next town," he tells them, "that I may preach there also, for that is why I came out."

Jesus did not give up his healing, or encountering the crowds, but in those quiet moments he re-centered his life in its original calling. Perhaps we could say that he clarified his vocation, and he clarified it in the only way we can ever clarify our true callings in life: in communion with our creator.

Beneath the frantic activity of your life is a deeper calling. You have a unique vocation and purpose in your life. But you can only discover what this is by disengaging to listen silently in prayer for God's presence with you.

I invite you to create a time of silent reflection in your life, because your busyness cannot accomplish the one thing that made a difference that night in Capernaum. No one can force you to go off alone to be with God. Like Jesus, you must find, within yourself, the wisdom to withdraw. When you do, you will discover the courage to go against the world that presses in and wants you to do otherwise. Your heavenly Father awaits you.

~~~

In the crush
of your hectic life,
in the scurrying,
the accomplishing,
the draining exhaustion,
may you receive
the wisdom to withdraw.

God So Loved the World

Raising children can be the most exhilarating, most confusing, most frustrating, most challenging, most demoralizing activity one can imagine. Those who have ventured forth into this perplexing activity wouldn't trade the opportunity for anything, except perhaps the knowledge of how these kids will turn out. If it weren't for the fact that childless folk also seem, in late age, to acquire grey hair, I would be convinced that rearing children, rather than aging, is the major cause for the silver film that overtakes our heads.

Everyone who dares to venture into childrearing always has a host of people willing to give advice. Back in my earlier childrearing days, it was Dr. Benjamin Spock and his homey handbook, *Baby and Child Care*. Then along came James Dobson's *Dare to Discipline* and a host of others. The past fifty years or so has been replete with handbooks and articles written to calm the doubts and assuage the fears of those who take the toughest of risks to peace and serenity, namely, to have children.

In the last analysis, however, despite all the advice about enhancing a child's self-esteem, rewarding behavior, and cultivating morality, many parents fall back upon what comes most naturally, and many children are raised by that familiar system of reward and punishment. Do well, my child, and you will win my favor. Do evil, my child, and you will incur my wrath. And, for the most part, children survive and adapt and are able to function in a society that operates on the same principles.

But there comes a time when all that begins to break down. The reward/punish model may work well for keeping society civil, but somewhere in our adulthood, as we begin to ponder our destinies and reflect upon the content of our lives, we become painfully aware that there is really little inside of us that is worth rewarding. There is little that would curry the favor of a parent, much less God. This awareness does not arrive through hell-fire preaching or books we read. Rather, we gradually come to know, in the depth of those hidden and unspoken places of our inner life, that there is something not good about us. Something that is dark. Something we would rather hide from everyone, particularly ourselves. To become human and to become mature is to recognize that burden we carry deep inside ourselves.

And so we condemn ourselves. That sounds harsh, doesn't it? But this really is what we do. I know that, because I am human and because I have entered deeply into many lives. This harsh judgment we pass upon ourselves leads us into all kinds of inappropriate behavior that can, in the last analysis, be reduced simply to our deepest inner cry of, "Love me. Pay attention to me."

Perhaps you have seen the bumper sticker: "Read the Bible. It'll scare the hell out of you." But I very much doubt that you need to have the hell scared out of you. Most of us are already frightened enough. Many of us are scared to death much of the time wondering what others think of us, knowing — or at least believing — that if they really knew us, they would discover our deepest, darkest secrets, and we would be judged. Now I know many people do a pretty good job of appearing unjudged, at least on the surface. But our chemical dependency, our inability to enter into painful situations that make us feel vulnerable, the superficiality of many of our relationships, and our self-indulgences are symptoms of our inner pain, borne from our self-judgment.

No, we don't need to read the Bible to have the hell scared out of us or to be judged, because we are experts at that. But we do need to read the Bible in order to hear that most of what we think about ourselves is not accurate, and what is accurate is not cause for despair. Ponder these words: *For God so loved the world that He gave His only Son, that whoever believes in Him should not perish, but have eternal life.*

Do you know why this is such a familiar and beloved verse of scripture? It is because there is no word of judgment. No condescension. This verse speaks of God as pure love, and it resonates with our deepest awareness that nothing can ultimately undo the judgment we bring upon ourselves other than pure, unbounded love. This love for you asks for nothing. This love does not coerce you to accept it. There are no threats, no bargains. This love asks only that you trust it. Believe it.

And how vast is this love that springs forth from the heart of God? It is vast enough to encompass, not only the world, but vast enough to embrace you in your darkness. The whole cosmos is centered — anchored — in that love.

The Christian faith, in order to describe what this love is like, has turned to the image of a parent and a child. Theologian and author Frank Seilhamer once said, "There are some things for which I am willing to risk or take a stand, and there are a few people for whom I am willing to risk my life and die. But there is no one for whom I am willing or able to sacrifice the life of my child." It is impossible to imagine such a love, isn't it? Yet that is precisely what God did for the likes of you and me, to deliver us from our debilitating shadows and to shed light on our darkened way.

The symbol of our faith is the cross. It is never far from us. Let us behold the cross, and the One who mounts that cross, in faith. This is God's final statement for us. Not that we are judged, not that we are to condemn ourselves, but that we are loved. Deeply loved. So deeply that God would endure the ultimate agony in love for us, and transform it into a cause for joy.

~~~

*May you have the courage
to gather up your pain,
your shame,*

your insecurity,
and your guilt,
and lay them down at the
feet of the One
who is pure love.
May you claim
the healing that awaits you.

Gentle Words of Divine Kindness

When I was about six years old, my step-grandfather, an Englishman who worked for the Baltimore and Ohio Railway as a conductor, died of a coronary attack. It was a more frequent practice in those days to display the body in its coffin and hold a visitation in the living room of the family home. So that's what we did. There he was, in our living room, his coffin surrounded by flowers, and for three nights family and friends crowded into the house to catch a last glimpse of Jack Scorer. The night after the funeral, the living room now vacant, my exhausted family went to bed early. In the deep hours of the night, when all was still, there was a sudden loud crash in the living room. It sounded like the roof had caved in. Terrified, we rushed down the stairs to the living room and beheld the carpet covered with plaster. The plaster ceiling had fallen—simply collapsed—covering the room with dust.

You can imagine what terror this aroused in a little six-year-old who had been living, eating, and sleeping in a home that nurtured his dead grandpa. My heart wouldn't stop pounding. And to this day, you might notice that when I enter a new room for the first time, I always look up to see if the ceiling is sagging!

Jesus is visiting a home. He is in a living room bursting with people, and a massive crowd has gathered at the door outside. His reputation as one who cared and as a healer is still drawing throngs to the doorstep. As he stands in the living room, quietly talking to those who are pressing in upon him, a few cakes of mud from the ceiling go *splat* on the floor next to him. Then some pebbles and twigs come sailing down. Suddenly, a huge section of the roof collapses down into the living room next to Jesus, followed by a man on a stretcher and his four comrades, all of them tumbling through the huge hole in the ceiling. Needless to say, Jesus is stunned, if not likewise terrified. Before him on the mat lies a paralyzed person.

But when he sees the persistent determination of the person's four friends, Jesus quietly says to this quadriplegic man, "My child, your sins are forgiven." With these few words, Jesus grabs hold of the common assumption that tragic circumstances are somehow the result of personal sin and the response of a punitive God, and he severs it.

However, these few gentle words of divine kindness, "My child, your sins are forgiven," precipitate a bitter controversy with the scribes. These few words of divine kindness, which reveal the will of God for forgiveness and reconciliation in all human relationships, challenge the human assumption that life is to be ordered by revenge, rather than forgiveness and reconciliation. So Jesus responds: "C'mon folks, which is easier: to say to this man, 'Rise and walk, or...your sins are forgiven?'" Rarely, if ever, in human history has a paralyzed person stood up on command and walked. That's how difficult forgiveness is. Rarely has a totally innocent person hung on a cross and been raised from the dead.

What has been the major disease that has afflicted humankind over the centuries? The bubonic plague? AIDS? Smallpox? No! It is revenge and its expression in violence. What has been the greatest weapon of mass destruction over the ages? An atomic bomb? Anthrax? No! It is revenge and its expression in violence.

More have suffered over the ages—more innocents have died over the ages—because we are diseased. We are in bondage to sin and cannot free ourselves, as we confess at each time of worship. The story of murderous and vengeful Cain and innocent Abel is the Bible's way of revealing to us how all of our relationships—whether as spouses or parents or children or associates or nations—are caught in the paralyzing disease of vengeance and cycles of violence. Jesus reminds us that it may be easier to make a quadriplegic move his or her limbs upon command and to walk, than to forgive one another from the heart. Forgive us our trespasses as we forgive the trespasses of others.

How often have you stood at a graveside, watching a family reconciled, after years of being alienated from one another by revenge? How often have you seen marriages turn to dust because, deep in the dark side of the human heart, is a desire for revenge? How often have you witnessed nations crippled by their leadership's desire for vengeance? There is only one way to cease the cycle of violence that paralyzes and leads ultimately to death: My child, your sins are forgiven!

But to forgive others, we must first be forgiven. To be freed from the disease that paralyzes us, we must first be forgiven *and forgive ourselves.* Martin Luther was so fond of this particular pastoral guidance that he recommended it as the foundation of the spiritual life: When you rise in the morning from your bed, make the sign of the cross and remember your baptism. It is in our baptism that we are reminded that God is a God of forgiveness and reconciliation, and that this is the foundation for the fullness of human life.

Have you noticed in your reading and listening to the scriptures how frequently, after Jesus has healed someone, he sends them home—back to their family? Do you suppose that Jesus is sending us back to our families? To our closest relationships? Do you suppose that he was on to something? We may not be able to influence the upsurge in vengeance and violence in this broken world, but we can go home, forgive, and live the life of reconciliation and new creation.

Well, the ceiling hasn't fallen—but forgiveness abounds. Let us live that life of grace.

~~~

Louis E. Bauer

May the promise of reconciliation
fill you with the desire
and the urgency
for forgiveness.
And may you be enfolded
in God's sweet grace.

Is That All There Is?

There is certain restlessness with life, something that used to be seen mainly amongst the young. But if you occupy my role, in which people feel free to share some of their deepest yearnings, today you also hear a number of older people sharing this same restlessness with life. So whether you are aged and achieved or are still young and only halfway down the achievement highway, you hear the same kind of restlessness. It is best summed up in that brief but penetrating question of the heart: *Is that all there is?*

The symptoms of this restlessness — not the cause, mind you, but the *symptoms* of this restlessness — are easily recognized: tossing in the night, boredom with one's family or one's marriage or one's job. A fundamental dissatisfaction that won't go away, no matter how much you might drink or how many drugs you might ingest or how tightly you may cram a schedule with activity so that you don't have to face the terror of a moment alone with yourself. And the collective symptoms of this restlessness

71

are most obvious in our society's lust for violence.

Now some would say that this basic restlessness is a luxury of the affluent and that the majority of people in the world haven't time to be bored—simple survival is their all-consuming concern in life. But it doesn't seem that this "restlessness with life" can really be reduced to simply having or not having. Like its symptoms, this restlessness runs far deeper.

You see, we humans were not created to plod through life like captives in a desert of the flesh. Humankind was created to swim in the rushing current of the world of the spirit. If you deny that world of the spirit, repress that world of the spirit, then someday the restlessness of your spirit will drive you to the question: Is that all there is?

Nicodemus had achieved. Nicodemus had accomplished. Nicodemus had arrived. But one dark night, tossing and turning in his sleep, he could take it no more. He had to have an answer to one question: Is that all there is? This older fellow, Nicodemus, was a member of the Jewish Supreme Court. He had his life sufficiently together, to all appearances, to be a responsible and esteemed leader of the Jewish community.

But now he comes, in the depth of the night, to meet with a homeless prophet and one-time carpenter who most likely spoke with a less than sophisticated accent.

No wonder he tiptoes out the back door — if we were Nicodemus, we would be rolling the car quietly down the driveway with the engine and the headlights off — to have a rendezvous with Jesus by the light of the moon. And little does he know that the pain of his restlessness this night will be his first cautious step into the thrilling and frightening world of truth — the world of the spirit.

Why did this person, a guardian of conventional religion and a pillar of the mainline church, show up on Jesus's doorstep that night? Was Nicodemus simply having a spiritual "sweet tooth," needing some sort of midnight snack with mysticism? Was he a dilettante, seeking to sit at the feet of the guru of the first century's version of a "new age" religion? Or did he show up at Jesus's doorstep with our question: Is that all there is?

Jesus invites him in. They converse. Jesus never answers Nicodemus directly. They are on two different planes, in two different worlds. Jesus speaks of the wind of the spirit, of being born from above, of starting life all over again from beyond.

Most people have a billiard ball view of reality, like Nicodemus. Hunched over the table with cue stick in hand, they poke one ball that hits another ball into the pocket. Do it right, and it'll happen every time. But life in a billiard ball world is suffocating. Jesus suggests that we are immersed and surrounded by a world of the spirit. We are restless until, in faith, we enter into this world surrounded and suffused by the spirit. A world that, in reality, tingles with God's passionate love affair with it—and with everyone of us—in this very moment.

Did Nicodemus take the plunge? Did he swim in the currents of another reality? Was he born again from above, a curious and spontaneous child, exploring with all his heart this new terrain, mapped by Jesus? Perhaps. It appears that he showed up with 100 pounds of spices to anoint the body after his leader's crucifixion. One legend says that Peter and John baptized him. Another legend tells us that he was kicked off the Jewish Supreme Court and banished from Jerusalem for his fascination with Jesus. And still another legend says that his body was found buried in a common tomb with

St. Stephen. Only legends, but they fit with a person who has begun to see and live in a different world—reborn into the realm of the spirit and healed of his restlessness.

Are you restless with your life? God does speak to us, if we dare listen to the symphony of the spirit. Nicodemus doesn't hear all the notes immediately—it will take him the rest of his life to get comfortable with the new dance in the presence of another reality. There just aren't any quick injections of spirituality that can inoculate us from this dis-ease. All Jesus can do is to offer himself as partner with us, inviting us to take a bold leap of faith into the realm of the spirit.

Are you really restless with your life? Do you want to risk the thrill and the joy of being reborn from above? Does this question resonate with you: Is that all there is? Then open your heart to the world of the spirit, to this fiery, purposeful love of Jesus—and let the wind blow you where it will, for this wind is the breath of God!

~~~

When your life is frayed
and your dusty dreams

have drifted away,
may the freshening spirit,
the breath of God,
lift you to the joy of new life.

Comfort for God's Children

There are three words in the English language that, when spoken, change human history. The power of these three little words to alter the course of life and to send people on exciting and challenging adventures is enormous. Have you been able to guess what those three little words are? I'm sure you have spoken them at some time in your life. Perhaps many times. The three words that have the power to transform life and change history are: I love you. I love you!

How many times have you spoken these words to someone? How many times have you meant it? How many times have you been willing to take the risks that accompany these words, when spoken in pure honesty?

A young man says to a young woman, "I love you." And the world has profoundly changed—for everyone. I know what this is like because I once said these words over hand cut roses to a young woman I hardly knew. And I keep saying them, even though the flowers may sometimes be dandelions. But like anyone who has ever fallen deeply in love (and isn't that an interesting term?), over the years I learned to use those words with some caution. You see, I thought I knew what love was. Years of experience of living with other people have taught me that I am only beginning to learn the meaning of love. And what that love is, I've discovered, has little to do with what I thought it was when I first uttered those words.

Before Jesus mounted the cross, he drew his disciples to him and uttered these farewell words: "Little children, a new commandment I give you, that you love one another, even as I have loved you." He did not give them a piece of advice, such as, "Gosh, guys, it sure would be nice if you worked together after I am raised from the dead." Nor, "Well, fellows, if you promise to work together, I'll tell the Father what neat people you are." Nor did he send them off to read some pop-psychology about self-esteem, assertiveness training, or how to win and influence a few friends. No, he gave his friends a commandment. An order. Basically: these are your marching orders now, for the rest of your lives. Non-negotiable, and to be obeyed. If you are going to be my disciple, then this is a requirement. Jesus cuts through all the baggage of life with his fierce compassion. He dares to make a new commandment...for *us*. His little children.

And the new commandment sounds simple, doesn't it? "That you love one another." I imagine that Jesus may have paused for a moment, thoughts racing through his head. These precious little children, throughout all ages to come...do they, will they know what love means? How can I show them?

So, for his little children, he said it a second time. And to make sure that all his children down through the ages would understand, he adds a word picture for them to keep looking at: "Even as I have loved you, that you should love one another." You mean Peter ought to love Andrew and Matthew and Bartholomew that way? Is that possible? Jesus knows his children well. He does believe that is possible.

"Love one another, as I have loved you!" Every disciple gathered around our Lord that day knew the meaning of those words, "As I have loved you." Every heart there leaped, as the memories of being genuinely cared for by Jesus flooded their minds. Each had been accepted and listened to when they poured out their life's stories and struggles. He didn't judge. Not once. He listened. He made them feel good about themselves. He saw them as capable people who could also love this deeply and live life this passionately. He had taught them about what few things mattered in life. He had comforted them. He had persuaded them not to be anxious. He had convinced them that God was in control of this world, even when all signs seemed to the contrary. He had shown them a love so broad and wide that it could encompass everyone and give them shelter from the stormy blasts.

He had loved them as one who was willing to do the unthinkable—to lay down his life for all his little children, then and down through the ages. Even for you! When you grasp the enormity of this love for you, you are comforted, freed, and empowered to say those three little words with a fullness of meaning you had never dared to believe would be possible.

~~~

This blessing comes to you
when your road is rough
and the companions are few.
With a whisper
that feels like an embrace

this blessing assures you
that you are capable,
you are acceptable,
you are loved.

Child of God

Child of God, you have been sealed by the Holy Spirit and marked with the cross of Christ forever.

A 32-ounce infant in the neonatal intensive care unit gasps to take air into her tiny lungs as the pastor touches her head with water and says, "...marked with the cross of Christ forever." A Somali student's blood baptizes the dusty ground as a voice from eternity whispers, "...marked with the cross of Christ forever." A young man stands perplexed and pained as a cherished relationship shatters into disappointment and bitterness, and a voice from beyond whispers, "Child of God...marked with the cross of Christ forever." An aged, frail body, all its energy spent in resisting the cancer, yields to its ravaging power as a voice from eternity whispers, "Child of God...marked with the cross of Christ forever."

Has there ever been a time in your life when you have longed to hear those assuring words? No matter who you are, no matter what you have done, no matter what pain you bear, no matter what fear paralyzes you and drives you to the brink, can you dare to believe them? Listen, Child of God! You have been marked with the saving cross of Christ. Forever.

Martin Luther, Philip Melanchthon, and those German princes who assembled in Augsburg, Germany five hundred years ago were our spiritual parents of the re-formation of the Church. Their confession of the faith affirmed that our baptisms are the whisper of the divine into the center of our hearts, so that before anything we ever do or think to do, we are marked with the cross of Christ forever. Quite simply, no matter what you have done to mess up your life, before whatever you may plan to straighten out your life, no matter what you think of yourself, no matter how much you may cover yourself with shame, you are a Child of God, marked with the cross of Christ forever. In other words, you are a precious child of eternity upon whom God will never give up. He cares about your destiny every bit as much as he cares about his own son.

There is a simple little mystery in the scriptures that is perhaps so obvious that it is concealed from us. Do you remember the story of Jesus's baptism in the River Jordan? The voice from heaven whispered (Or did it thunder?), "This is my beloved son in whom I am delighted." This took place immediately before Jesus commenced his life's work. Before he had done anything, accomplished anything, or failed at anything, his Father whispered in his ear the words that would accompany him through the saddest and loneliest life ever lived: You are my beloved son in whom I am delighted! Never forget that, Jesus. Never forget that. Perhaps the fleeting memory of those very words, as his life blood drained away, empowered him to surrender confidently: Into your hands, Father, I commit my spirit.

"Christen" is a centuries-old word often used at a baptism. That word has to parts: *Christ* and *en*, which means "to make." When we whiten a wall, we make it white. When God christened you, He made you a part of Christ, and into your heart God whispers, if you will but listen: "Child of God...marked with the cross of Christ forever." In this very act, God has assured you that he will never allow you to suffer anything more than Christ has suffered, nor receive anything less than Christ has received.

In the spirit of those German princes who confessed their faith in Augsburg, trust that. Trust the God of the waters of baptism.

~~~

May the refreshing water of your baptism
drench you with the assurance
that no matter how far you have strayed
or how long you have wandered,
you have been sealed by the Holy Spirit
and marked with the cross of Christ
forever.

The Question

*T*here is silence. The place is lonely, far from the pressing needs of humanity. Jesus is praying. He whispers toward heaven, beyond the range of their hearing, so they sit here serenely, embraced by the silence. The whispering ceases and he turns to them, a question forming on his lips.

Something happens whenever he asks them a question. It is always somehow more than a question in search of an answer. His questions seem to make answers happen. Yes, that's it. His questions, rather than perplexing them, always seem to reveal answers. It intrigues the disciples, this mystery. His questions appeal directly to their hearts, never their heads, and engage the deepest, most hidden corners of their lives. There is always more power in his questions than their answers can ever offer. When he asks questions, somehow the world is never quite the same for them.

And now another of his questions is forming in space, hurtling toward them like a meteor, burning its pathway into their hearts.

"Who do people say that I am?" he asks. Again, a moment of silence. They stare at one another, exchanging knowing glances. Each of them knows that he is asking something far greater than any one of them cares to answer.

The disciples wrack their brains, hiding their hearts, and slough off the question with this answer: "Some say you are John the Baptist. Others say you are Elijah. Others say one of the great old prophets." Multiple choice answer, Jesus. Don't ask me to answer your question, because I am afraid. I am afraid because I know what you are asking me and I know what you are asking *of* me.

You know, contrary to what we have been told, the disciples were actually good listeners. Luke tells us that they repeat, word for word, what the crowds were saying about this itinerant rabbi: "Now Herod the tetrarch heard about all that was going on. And he was perplexed because some were saying that John had been raised from the dead, others that Elijah had appeared, and still others that one of the prophets of long ago had come back to life. But Herod said, 'I beheaded John. Who, then, is this I hear such things about?' And he sought to see him." *He sought to see him.* Can you imagine what might have happened had this ruthless dictator succeeded in seeing Jesus? Would he have beheaded him with all the terror our modern world knows all too well? Or might he have become his disciple?

But we are avoiding the question. Not unlike the disciples' response—some say this, some say that—we mouth our answers in creeds and rituals, as if we think we can somehow keep him in our heads, at a safe distance from our hearts. How often do we wrap him up, all cozy in our church's programs, and stash him safely in the corner, so as not to interfere with our more important business? As if there isn't any more important business in life than to answer the one relentless question he asks.

And now the silence is shattered, but this time with that frightening, awesome question from which so many of us, including the disciples, have been seeking to hide: "But who do *you* say that I am?" And if your heart is not racing right now, then something is wrong, because he is standing here. Right here and right now. And he is asking you, "But who do *you* say that I am? And somehow you know that the creeds or a glib answer from your head won't do. And everything you may have ever learned in Sunday School somehow fails, because you are standing on holy ground that is shaking. God's relentless, all consuming love struggles to elbow its way into your little world, your trembling little heart. This love seeks to heal you, to lift your burden, to give you a vocation and a purpose in what is otherwise an empty life of chasing idols.

Yes, it frightens me when he asks me his question, because I know what he wants of me and for me. But his question is as gentle as his person. Remember—his questions reveal answers. He asks, not for his sake, but for ours. His questions heal. They open our sin-blinded eyes and our pain-filled hearts to a love that loves us more than we love ourselves. This is a love that loves you if you haven't made it in the world because there isn't any room for you, just as there wasn't any room for him at the inn. This is a love that forgives you and teaches you how to forgive others, even when you cannot seem to forgive yourself. This is a love that will not and cannot speak or act violently under any circumstance, even when what is most precious to him is spilling his life blood on a cross. He is love, pure love.

Peter's heart bursts, and he shouts, "You are the Messiah, the Son of the living God!" Immanuel. God-with-us. It is Christmas again, in all its joy and richness. But Peter can only answer for himself, as Jesus stands there, inquiring down through the ages until this very moment in your life. "Who do you say that I am?"

He is asking you now. This moment. Do you dare to answer him from your heart, not your head? Do not be frightened. He and his Father want to be with you. All he can give you is a cross, his Father's love, and his promise to be with you — next to you, in front of you, behind you — to the end of the ages. And it is enough. It is all you will ever need. So, not for God's sake, but for your sake, answer his question. Give him the only thing you have to give away. Give him your heart.

~~~

When the question
enters into you,
may you have the courage of Peter,
and may the gentle love of the questioner
find its way into your heart.

Signs on the Journey

*W*hen I was a child, a favorite Sunday afternoon pastime was a drive into the country. As my father drove us through little towns with pretty houses and neatly manicured lawns and flower beds, I would sometimes wonder what it would be like to live in such a pleasant place. I invite you to travel with me down one of those country roads. We'll keep a close eye on the traffic signs to guide us. So tighten your seat belt, and let's hit the road.

We are traveling down this picturesque road to a town called Nain. And there's the sign: "Turn Right. 15 miles to Nain, A Pleasant Place to Live." That's the meaning of the word Nain: a pleasant place. Kind of a little Eden. As a pleasant place, it reminds us of all our yearnings for the good life: little traffic, cleanly swept streets, time to chat with passersby, gardens full of roses, parks for the children to play in. Nain, the pleasant place to live, touches our yearnings and desires for the wholesomeness and beauty of simple, uncluttered living. This little town feels like a symbol of the goodness of life because, in this pleasant place to live, life is good to us.

So we make our turn, and proceed to the pleasant place. But suddenly another sign looms as you and I enter Nain: "Dead End." The announcement reminds us of all the detours and disappointments in life. It reminds us that what seems like Eden, a pleasant place to live, is really a place of pain, sorrow, and death. Our feelings about the goodness of life are thrown into deepest question by this sign that has brought us to a halt. Dead end. Can anyone give us directions?

Jesus was entering Nain, the pleasant place to live, with a crowd of followers. This place was so close to Nazareth that he had played there as a boy. He may have even known the woman he was about to meet. Suddenly he encounters a familiar Dead End sign. A funeral procession is passing by, bearing the lifeless body of a young man whose grieving mother is leading the procession. What is about to unfold is one of the profoundest and most deeply moving encounters between God and a human being anywhere in the scriptures. First we are told the biography of a person whom God is about to embrace.

She was a widow, Luke tells us, who led the grieving procession. She knew one of the deepest sorrows of life. Her beloved, with whom she had shared life, was gone. He had loved her, held her. He had helped to make Nain a pleasant place for her to live. He had died a few years ago. So she was not a woman unfamiliar with the loneliness of grief and life's tears. Studies of stress experiences in life rank the death of one's spouse as the highest.

But there is an even greater pain in life: the loss of a child. Nothing is more devastating. Nothing evokes deeper anger or deeper despair than the death of one's child. And here is the widow of Nain, leading the grieving procession for her only — her *only* — child. He in whom her husband still lived. And now even this precious child is dead.

And, of course, she was a woman, one whose inferior rank in the culture placed her with the slaves. A woman could not pray in the temple with a man. A rabbi could not demean himself by speaking to a woman in public, not even his wife, sister, or daughter. Women were blamed for death, because death was introduced into the world through Eve. Consequently, women were compelled to lead funeral processions. So this widow leads her procession, symbolizing the guilt and responsibility for the curse of death she and her type have brought down upon her husband and her only child.

There in the center of Nain, the pleasant place to live, trudges one who lives in unimaginable loneliness, unimaginable despair, unimaginable humiliation. At the heart of Nain looms the symbol: Dead End.

Through the crowds, through the tense emotion, Jesus's eyes peer into her heart. Of course, he must have had compassion. Sympathy. No. Even the priest who passed by the Samaritan on the road to Jericho was capable of that. Luke tells us that Jesus was *moved to the depths of his being*. The very foundation of God's heart is shaken. The love that created the universe is crushed by the sight of this suffering person. Jesus is moved, moved to do something. Compassion and sympathy watch. We feel sorry for the one who suffers. But Jesus is moved. He is hurtled into a course of action.

There, in the dust of a village road, divine love becomes a voice that speaks from eternity to the grieving woman, "Don't cry." And then a hand reaches out to touch the coffin, and a voice bellows so loudly his heavenly Father could hear, "Get up! Get up!" The same words of resurrection his Father would speak to him...and one day to you and me. "Get up!"

And taking the young man up in his arms, Jesus places him into his mother's arms, alive and whole.

We drive on from Nain today, you and I. Perhaps we have not yet known the depths of God's resurrection in our life, but we drive on, having seen that he wills to be with us. He shares our sorrow and disappointment. He desires to turn this creation again into a beautiful life, a pleasant place to live. As certainly as he has renewed the life of his only child, our Lord, God will renew our lives and those of our beloved.

We have passed through Nain now. No more Dead Ends. God has posted new signs for us to follow on our journey. The first says: Don't cry! The last says: Get Up!

~~~

*When your pleasant place
has become a place of suffering and sorrow,
may the compassionate voice of the One*

who knows your path
lift you into joy.

Blessed Are They Who Mourn

A number of years ago, the insurance industry conducted a study about life's stressful experiences. The industry was, of course, interested in learning which life experiences most significantly affected our health and longevity. The study revealed that the most stressful, painful life experience is the death of one's spouse. In other words, the ending of a deep, significant, loving relationship. On the basis of my experience as a pastor, I would also include the loss of any person to whom one is intimately close—especially a relative. The period of mourning for a spouse, a child, or a parent can last a very long time. To the bereaved person, it can feel like an eternity. The anguish of loss may diminish over time, but it never entirely disappears. If you have not yet experienced such a loss, I must tell you that you will. And it will feel as if your world has collapsed.

But the death of a loved one is not the only reason a person may mourn. That same study pointed out that moving to a new community is high on the list. Relationships, roles, sources of personal identity, friendships—all these are left behind. A person's roots within a community, both subtle and significant, are painfully axed. During the period of mourning what has been relinquished, a person can feel very much alone.

When we investigate more closely the darkened cloak of mourning, we will find other losses in life: the end of a marriage (no matter how painful the marriage may have been), a child's leaving home, and our own aging with its accompanying loss of strength, concentration, or memory.

Now you might respond, "But this is all part of life," and you would be absolutely correct. But to be correct, is also to be honest. And real honesty will compel you to admit how much you yourself have been touched by grief and mourning. Most of us do learn how to cope with our losses, to go on. But the hurt is still there. It is that dull ache just beneath the surface, rising up often when we least expect it.

I served for three years as a chaplain in a large federal psychiatric hospital and subsequently worked for another ten years with numerous discharged psychiatric patients. I have had the privilege of sharing people's deepest despair and feelings of desolation. What I have learned over the years is that, except for those instances where the cause is genetic or biochemical, much of mental illness has, as its foundation, grief, mourning, or painful loss. You might understand, then, why I consider the Beatitude, "Blessed are they who mourn, for they shall be comforted," (Matt. 5:4) one of Jesus's most powerful promises.

I have worked with many dying people, and I have yet to encounter one who had not accepted death. So often this acceptance is much easier for the dying person than it is for the family and friends who know they will soon be plunged into grief and mourning. Sadly, the society in which most of us live seems most uncomfortable with bereavement. These days, we often have memorial services for those who have died. Even the word "funeral" has become a tad unseemly. As a result, we tend not to know how to offer comfort for someone deep in grief.

What really underlies the experience of mourning, to which Jesus directs his promise of comfort? What makes this fundamental life experience so painful? We may need to look deep within ourselves for the answer. Let me suggest that when we lose someone to death, we feel as if we have lost part of ourselves. We have lost someone through whom we knew who we were, through whom we were accepted, affirmed, and cherished. One of the biggest mistakes we make in life is to fail to understand how deeply we are connected to one another and how dependent we are upon one another for our emotional existence.

So what about this comfort of which the Good Shepherd speaks? He tells his disciples: In my Father's house are many rooms. I go to prepare a place for you, so that where I am, you will be also. It's a place where everyone may be together again, restored and renewed. A place where we are fully known for who we are. Jesus speaks of it in the imagery of a good family. Life with a good parent.

Jesus does not suggest that there will not be grief and mourning in life. His Beatitude affirms this honestly as a very real experience all of us will encounter. But he does promise that this is not the last word. *His word* is the last and final word!

Comfort for life's mourning comes from seeing one's life by way of the cross and the resurrection. Jesus never forgot that his life was a road back to eternity. The life of our Lord is a reminder to each one of us that our life, too, is a journey back to eternity. We tend to be so busy with many things and sometimes overwhelmed with so many demands. When you grieve a loved one, you may be told, with every good intention: keep busy! Perhaps it would help to pause long enough to mourn honestly. In doing so, you may indeed discover the blessedness that comes from being comforted by the Lord of Life.

~~~

On the day when you shatter
into shards of deepest grief,
and the fabric of your life
is ripped into pieces,
this blessing comes with comfort,
speaking no words,
but sitting beside you,
knowing, hearing, loving, and
enfolding you.

Where We Find Answers

One of the greatest privileges and sacred responsibilities of a pastor is to be a counselor. A spiritual guide to people. And one of the most challenging and difficult questions that people bring to a pastor is this: How can I know what the will of God is for my life? It's the kind of question that gets asked often by people who earnestly struggle with careers, families, marriages, vocations, and relationships. And it's interesting that the question almost always ends with those words, "for my life."

The emphasis on *my life* reminds a pastor that the questioner has entrusted her or his life to the guidance of the pastor, an awesome responsibility. I suppose the reason people come to pastors with that question is they assume the pastor has wrestled with that crucial life question. And they would be right. Most pastors have indeed struggled with that question. But the roadmaps for the journey of what God wills for my life are not easy to provide to the questioner. Most people are hoping for clear, if not easy, answers, but all I can do is offer a story. You see, stories are the Bible's way (and they were always Jesus's way) of answering the questions you might be asking in the silence of your heart.

There was once a man named Terah who lived in a strange place called Ur of the Chaldees. He had three sons, and yearned for a richer life. One of his sons died, and he decided to set forth on a long journey to another land. It's not unusual for the loss of a loved one or an important relationship to propel us in a different direction, to take another road in our life's journey. We don't know for sure if that was what set Terah packing from Ur with his two sons, Abraham and Nahor, and their wives to the land of Canaan. Was he running from his grief?

The Bible says that Terah never reached this land of promise, that place of new beginnings. He stopped at Haran with his family and settled there. He made a compromise when he ended his journey at Haran. The promise of a new future would have to wait for someone in the next generation who was running toward something, rather than away from something, as Terah was.

One afternoon, the question reverberated in the chambers of Abraham's heart: How can I know what the will of God is for my life? And a voice said: Pack up your bags, Abraham, son of Terah. Leave your country. Leave your kindred and family. Leave your father's house and begin your journey to the place I will show you.

Tear up your roots, Abraham! Nothing could be more wrenching for a person in the ancient world than to do what the Lord had just commanded. There were no telephones by which Abraham could phone home, no postal service to deliver a letter with a cry for help. The Lord's command meant throwing everything to the wind. It meant becoming a wanderer, trusting a dream and believing a promise that was, even now, becoming faint, even illusory.

You have probably noticed that what the Lord said to Abraham was not exactly an answer to his question. In fact, in its incredible vagueness, it was hardly an answer at all. Instead, it was an imperative. A command to obey and respond in trust to what seemed to be an impossible promise. "Go to the land I will show you." The Lord doesn't even tell Abraham where he is going, but he makes a promise to

Abraham that strikes the old man where he is most vulnerable.

Now Abraham was getting up in years. He was about 75, which sounds a bit old to be out cavorting in the countryside in search of dreams and promises, when he might have remained at home, enjoying the dignity and comfort due him in his old age. And have you ever noticed, in your reading of the Hebrew Bible, that God likes to make journeys with older folks? He likes to remind us that life is not finished. Older people's lives are not washed up quite as soon as some younger folk might think. God seems to delight in an old man asking, "What is your will for my life?"

But what is Abraham's particular vulnerability? He has no offspring. Sarah, his wife, is infertile. Abraham and Sarah have no children to love, no grandchildren to delight them in their old age, no progeny who will take care of them in their final years. They have tried everything, including the surrogate mother route with Abraham's other wife, Hagar, but that didn't turn out so well. But the Lord has made an incredible promise to Abraham that he will be a father of nations.

So, not knowing where he is going, following a dream that is a biological impossibility, an old man packs up his belongings on the back of a camel, ventures forth with his two wives and his nephew, and hits the divine road. Why did he do it? What answer had he found? All the Bible ever tells us is that he believed. He trusted. An elderly gentleman, setting forth on a divine journey, riding toward the rising, not the setting, sun.

And you know what? That was enough for God. The Bible tells us that God particularly likes these kinds of people who live that way, who don't need all the blueprints or road maps or a cosmic grand design. God says, "These are my kind of people!" People who will venture forth, knowing he is taking them somewhere, trusting that he can be depended upon to sustain them, and confident they will see things they have never seen before.

Abraham thought he was setting off for a new home in a new country, but what happened is that he went down in history as a bold adventurer and a person of faith. A model of trust. And God liked him—just for that. It was his faith that pleased God, not anything Abraham had done, because Abraham was actually rather weak-willed. He had pawned his wife off to pharaoh to save his neck, and had kicked his second wife out because Sarah became jealous of her. But the old man had faith, and God loved him for that.

The problem with that question we so often ask—How can I know what the will of God is for my life—is that asking the question is stalling. That's why we need to hear stories of people like Abraham who have grasped that God is a God of movement. People in the Bible are always on the move. God is not a God of rest. He goes with people who set out on journeys, including the boldest journey from Bethlehem to Jerusalem to the hill of the cross, reminding us that he even accompanies us to eternity. So let's stop stalling and get moving, children of Abraham.

~~~

Lord God, you have called your servants
to ventures of which we cannot see the ending,
by paths as yet untrodden,
through perils unknown.
Give us faith to go out with good courage,
not knowing where we go,

but only that your hand is leading us
and your love supporting us;
through Jesus Christ, our Lord. Amen.

-Eric Milner-White (1884-1963)

Floating in the Sea of God

Watching a tiny infant being taught to swim is truly a remarkable experience. One is amazed — even horrified — to see these little tykes almost tossed into the water to fend for themselves. They seem to have an innate ability, which they will lose later in their lives, to float. Maybe learning to float through life is something we all need to learn how to do. Note that I do not advocate drifting through life. No, floating is something quite different. You have probably heard that whenever there is an accident at sea or on a lake, the safest thing to do is to float or to hang onto something that floats until someone comes to the rescue. Those who perish are often the poor souls who thrash about wildly, trying to swim to shore. They become exhausted. And sink.

Now, perhaps the title of this meditation is becoming a little more comprehensible: Floating in the Sea of God. Let me suggest, for your contemplation, that faith means floating in the sea of God.

The Sea of Galilee, not very far from where Jesus grew up, is as dangerous as it is beautiful. Located 680 feet below sea level, the land around the sea has a fertile climate that is almost tropical. The hills surrounding the sea, which is the scene of a terrifying episode in the lives of the disciples, are carved deep with ravines and gorges that act like gigantic funnels, drawing the cold winds toward the sea. In a matter of seconds, out of the clear, blue sky, the calm surface of the water can become a churning cauldron.

Jesus had worked hard that day, teaching, healing, listening, and talking, all in the heat of the sun. Now, in the cool of the evening, he had invited his disciples to travel to the other side of the sea in their little boat. They were not alone in their journey. Mark tells us that they were part of a flotilla of little fishing boats.

And then suddenly, out of that clear, blue sky (and isn't that the way it is in life?), the sea is whipped up by a fierce gale. The water churns and seethes with danger, and the waves heave over the edge of the fragile craft. The disciples frantically bale water, terrified that at any moment they will be overcome by the tempest.

And where was Jesus, amidst this turmoil? He was in the back of the boat, resting. Mark tells us he was sleeping, his head upon a pillow. I love this picture! Here is Jesus, totally at rest and totally vulnerable during the tempest. He is floating in the sea of God. Is this not the ultimate example of faith, entrusting oneself to the care of God? Jesus knew well the ways of this sea. He lived near it. He knew how quickly life could be thrown into churning and upheaval.

Some of the disciples run to the back of the boat to rouse Jesus. It is not as apparent as we might suppose what they expected from him or why they turned to him. Did they see him as another warm body who could help them bale water from the boat? Certainly, they had seen him a number of times healing people and ridding them of their illnesses. They had seen him do incredible things, but never had they witnessed what was about to happen.

Jesus does respond to the disciples, but his response is not to grab a bucket or to comfort them. No, his response is to directly encounter the forces raging out of control creating this threatening maelstrom on the Sea of Galilee. "Peace! Be still!" he says. From the centeredness of a heart anchored in the heart of God, God's peace and tranquility are imparted to the churning sea, until it once again becomes placid. The same peace in the heart of Jesus as he slept on the pillow becomes the peace that dawns on the sea at dusk in Galilee.

And then Jesus asks a powerful question, "Why are you so afraid? Do you still have no faith?" Only the floater in the sea of God can really grasp how provocative that question is. And that same question is put to each of us on our voyage through this life.

Father Thomas H. Green, in his marvelous book, *When the Well Runs Dry*, describes the kind of faith that is like floating in the sea of God, just as Jesus floated that evening in the boat: "Everything," Father Green says, "literally everything, is in God's hands. When we realize this—realize it experientially—we have truly learned to float. Deep down, we know, and are happy in the knowledge, that the life of floating which has begun will last for eternity."

Floaters in the sea of God never swim again, nor do they have any desire to do so. The wonders of floating fill their every desire. If only those around us, those brothers and sisters we love—some swimming strenuously, some clinging to rafts of their own making, some building huts to settle on the shore—could realize that floating is the only answer! But even that is the Lord's concern. What he has done for floaters, he will surely do for others, if only they let him. Since he waited so long for us, he will surely wait for them. In the meantime, our floating may be a sign, a sacrament of what can be.

Is this our prayer: Lord, teach us how to float? I am convinced that before we pray that prayer, from the secret corner of our hearts, we need to know something the disciples may have missed in Jesus's invitation that tempestuous evening. I wonder if they really heard Jesus when he said, "Come, let us go over to the other side." You cannot truly float in the sea of God until you have been grasped by a vision of where the journey is headed. You will continue to swim and thrash and struggle about in life's waters until you are grasped by the destination for all of this floating, which is nothing less than eternity! But when you know that life's destiny is eternity, floating in the sea of God becomes natural, like breathing. You are buoyed by faith. Whether your life's waters are placid and calm or heaving and churning, you will float toward eternity, your heart shaped by the words of him

whom even the wind and waves obey: "Peace.
Be Still."

~~~

In your life's journey,
when the tempest and turmoil appear,
may you know peace,
may you be still,
and may you be buoyant.
May you float.

Put to the Test

Then Jesus was led up by the Spirit into the wilderness to be tempted by the devil. [2] He fasted forty days and forty nights, and afterwards he was famished. [3] The tempter came and said to him, "If you are the Son of God, command these stones to become loaves of bread." [4] But he answered, "It is written, 'One does not live by bread alone, but by every word that comes from the mouth of God.'" [5] Then the devil took him to the holy city and placed him on the pinnacle of the temple, [6] saying to him, "If you are the Son of God, throw yourself down; for it is written,

'He will command his angels concerning you' and 'On their hands they will bear you up, so that you will not dash your foot against a stone.'" [7] Jesus said to him, "Again it is written, 'Do not put the Lord your God to the test.'" [8] Again, the devil took him to a very high mountain and showed him all the kingdoms of the world and their splendor; [9] and he said to him, "All these I will give you, if you will fall down and worship me." [10] Jesus said to him, "Away with you, Satan! for it is written, 'Worship the Lord your God, and serve only him.'" [11] Then the devil left him, and suddenly angels came and waited on him.
Matthew 4:1-11

I have stood at the foot of the Mount of Temptation, and I have personally seen the setting for Jesus's encounter with, and testing by, the power of evil. It is a godawful lonely place, even two thousand years later. It is an eerie place where the winds swirl above the Dead Sea, howling at times like the furies. It is also a place of tremendous beauty in its starkness and barrenness. A tranquil place. A place where you can go forty days without hearing any sound, except for the winds. It is a place where you can truly be alone, where you can think, reflect, purge yourself of your daily concerns, and open your heart to God. But this is also a place where loneliness sets in, and where there is loneliness, there is danger. There is hard testing of who we really are.

So that is the geographic and emotional context of this profound struggle between good and evil. The story you read above from the Gospel of Matthew has such an aura of otherworldliness, doesn't it? It's hard to imagine yourself locked in the same kind of struggle as Jesus was, so you become a bystander cheering on the hero. You read the story (which you may have heard scores of times in your life) knowing that Jesus can handle himself out there in this godforsaken desert. After all, look at who he is. This strange story seems to have little to do with your life. This is all about Jesus, right?

And yet. Ponder this: we would know nothing of Jesus's testing in the wilderness unless he very specifically thought it had a great deal to do with us. After all, who witnessed the testing of Jesus? How did Matthew, Mark, and Luke come to know about it? There is only one way what happened to Jesus became known. He chose to share his experience with his disciples who remembered it and retold the story. Here was Jesus, very much the pastor, the caring person, taking aside his disciples one afternoon to share with them the profound struggles he had encountered and the weighty questions about his vocation with which he grappled. Perhaps the most searing question was that of self identify. *Who am I?*

The decision of Jesus to share this story with his friends meant that he was also sharing with them his deep struggle. He did not do this to impress or scare them. Rather, it was a way of comforting them, of cheering his little band of followers. We all know that nothing can be more comforting than when someone can say to us, "I know what you have experienced. I know how you have been hurt. I know what it is like…because I have been there, too."

When you are hurting or doubting yourself, you don't need someone to take away your pain or offer reassuring platitudes. What you need is someone with whom you can share it. Someone who knows from experience what you are going through. Jesus's sharing the story of his testing was his way of saying to anyone who comes to seek him out, "My friend, I know what you are experiencing, because I have been there, too."

Prior to his forty days in the godforsaken wilderness, Jesus had just had another life changing experience. He was chilled to the bone, standing in the mud of the frigid waters of the Jordan River with his cousin, John the Baptist, when eternity parted and the heavens announced, "This is my beloved son in whom I am well pleased!" Startling words to the young carpenter of Nazareth who himself had something to say that the world needed to hear. It is likely the same thing was said of you, at a time you no longer remember. But you, too, have been so named and identified. Indeed, the same precious words and a few dribbles of water have named you, and you are as dear a child of God as the one who was his son.

We forget that so easily. Many of us spend our lives trying to make something of ourselves, to our own pain and frustration. We yield to doubt. We become vulnerable to the evil one whose favorite entry into our lives is to tempt us to doubt just that—who we are and whose we are.

No sooner is Jesus baptized with those self-affirming words, than immediately, according to the Bible, he is put into that wilderness of life, being tested. And the testing is dramatic: hunger, power, miracles, and empires all in one's control. But beneath all this testing, only one question is really being asked: If you are the son of God...*If you are a child of God*?! My friend, is this not the one question behind all the tests, trials, and temptations of your life? It is posed for the singular purpose of engaging your doubt, doubting who you are and whether God cares. For when you doubt that, you are capable of anything.

The author of the Epistle to the Hebrews reminds us that Jesus knew every temptation a human being can know. He doubted his own self during those forty days in the wilderness. He knew what it was like to lose someone he loved, Lazarus, and he groaned in anger at the power of death. He knew what it meant to be betrayed by a friend. He knew what it was like to be frustrated with his dearest friends who would not listen and who hadn't the vaguest idea of what was poured out on a bloody cross.

But his response to that self doubt, that hidden questioning of whether the Father really cared, was to share with his disciples how he had responded to the evil one. By his sharing, he taught his disciples that the way through the testing and doubts of life was to keep their focus on God. To be obedient, even when they could not see clearly where they were going, when they doubted not only themselves, but the one who called them.

Matthew reminds us that the Spirit led Jesus through this testing. He leads you through your own testing. And angels are waiting to minister to you. Remember this: you have never been alone in the wilderness of life. There is one who is now, and always will be, with you. He is the one who told you who you are. His child. He will never abandon you.

~~~

In times of struggle and doubt,
when you feel stretched and stressed
and tested beyond your endurance,
may you recall who you are
and whose you are,
beloved child of God.

What Do You Expect?

They pushed and shoved that day to get into the synagogue. It's always a special day when people crowd a temple to listen to God's word, but today was extra special. Jesus had just returned to his home town, Nazareth of Galilee, to announce the message of God's nearness to life. Expectations ran high as this home town boy took his place in the synagogue. His reputation, since he'd left them, had grown. Now his friends and neighbors stood in awe of him, as they awaited his gracious words. Contrary to popular belief, the people of Nazareth were well bred folks, well educated, and reasonably affluent. This was a comfortable middle class town with just a few pockets of poverty. And, oh, they were so proud of their home town boy who'd made good.

When Jesus stood up to read from the scroll, he read a familiar text from Isaiah: The spirit of the Lord is upon me because he has anointed me:

to proclaim good news to the poor,
to proclaim freedom to prisoners,

to recover sight to the blind (vision to the downhearted),
to set at liberty those who are oppressed,
to announce the cancellation of all debts.

You could hear a pin drop, as a hush fell upon the expectant crowd. Then Jesus rolled up the scroll, gave it to an attendant, and sat down to preach his sermon, as was the custom.

If brevity, conciseness, and directness are the hallmarks of a great sermon, then you are about to hear history's greatest, most remarkable example of preaching: "Today this scripture has been fulfilled in your hearing." Amen.

"Amen?" That was it? This was perhaps the shortest sermon in history. No illustrations. No meandering. Totally Biblical. A one-liner. A shocker.

And how did the people that day in the synagogue respond to Jesus's trial sermon? Did they applaud? Fall asleep? Shake his hand and say, "Nice sermon, pastor?" No. They were outraged. In their anger they seized him, intending to drag him out of town to a hill and throw him down headlong. But he slipped away into the crowd. His hour had not yet come. But it would, eventually.

What had gone wrong? It was a brief little sermon. It was good news, spoken in love. A short description of his ministry, but met with resistance and anger. What had Jesus stirred up with his message about God's agenda in life?

It wasn't *just* that his sermon was blasphemous in his claiming God's identity. I believe we miss the mark and fail to grasp the depth of what he stirred up if we limit our assessment of what happened. Let's face it. Jesus's sermon was too much about social activism and social concerns. It was too political. His exegesis of Isaiah, combined with God's agenda, was clearly economic and deeply value-laden with God's bias toward the poor, the oppressed, and those financially indebted to the good folks of Nazareth. God's values clashed hard that day with those of the Nazarenes.

And not only that. Jesus dared to say *today*—not sometime in the distant future, but right now—his ministry and God's agenda were with the poor, the oppressed, the imprisoned, and the broken ones. You would think this would be good news, but it stirred up anger and disappointment. It still does, even in us, until we empty ourselves and open our hearts to God.

The expectations of Nazareth had been deeply disappointed because they had listened out of the needs of their own selves, rather than daring to open their hearts to God's good news. Their disappointment led to rejection of their home town boy.

All too often we painfully discover that God, or what we want God to be, does not meet our expectations. How about you? You may not even realize you are doing this. Do you expect God to reward good, hard-working people and punish those who aren't? Remember that the Lord himself reminds us that God makes the sun to shine on good and bad alike and gives rain to those who do good as well as those who do evil. He is God of astonishing forgiveness and love.

When illness and disease consume you, when you suffer heartbreaking disappointment or unbearable grief, do you ask, "Why is God allowing this to happen to me?" You are not alone. Faithful people expect God to shield them from life's pain. The reality is that this Jesus of Nazareth who said, "Lo, I am with you always," is one who, like you and me, in the words of Isaiah, was "...despised and rejected by humanity, a man of sorrows and acquainted with grief." He who knew the depths of suffering is the one who walks with you through the valley of the deepest shadows. He is *with* you. He does not stand above you and shout, "How are you doing down there?"

There was a time when many of Jesus's disciples turned away and no longer followed him because he did not speak and act in accordance with their expectations of the Messiah. Jesus even said to the twelve, "Do you also want to go away?" But Peter, who was beginning to listen for God, replied, "Lord, to whom shall we go? Yours are the words of eternal life."

If you are willing to exchange your fantasies about God and really listen, you will discover in his words one who is alive and waiting to empower you to believe in him, to believe in yourself, and to live with the courage with which he lived. If you can release your unrealistic expectations of yourself and other people, you will find that he is waiting to nourish you and strengthen you for growth and for life in this world, with all its joys, its sorrows, and its ambiguities. If you seek him in your workplace, your place of worship, your family, and your neighborhood, you will find that he has been there all the time, waiting for you, in the faces of your brothers and sisters.

~~~

May the sweetest breeze of courage
sweep away your false expectations,
so you may be
nurtured in love
and filled with hope.

What Do You See?

They went to Capernaum; and when the Sabbath came, he entered the synagogue and taught. They were astounded at his teaching, for he taught with authority. Mark 1:21-22

Let me invite you to ponder a question. You may find this question simplistic, and you may be quick to dismiss it, but I invite you to grab hold of this question with deep seriousness. To enter into it. The question is this: have you ever thought about what it would have been like to encounter Jesus during his brief life on this Earth? What would you have experienced when you entered the space around Jesus? Lest you think this is a trivial question that is easily answered, don't forget that the disciples were never fully clear in their minds and hearts about just who Jesus was, at least not through his earthly life.

What would you have seen, had you been one of the people in the crowd at the synagogue in Capernaum? One of the first images that may come to your mind is that of a man with a beard, long flowing hair, blue eyes, wearing a sparkling white robe, his face radiating compassion. This is an image many have. It comes to us through tradition and art. It is a Nordic Christ, one who might have been more at home in the colder climate of northern Europe.

You may have a different image of Jesus in mind, but the image I describe above tends to show us that there is a lot inside us that informs our perception of who Jesus is. Many people have a stereotype that they impose upon the person, rather than allowing the person to reveal himself to them. The danger in this is that you may come to create the Jesus that you want him to be, rather than allowing yourself to become what he wants you to be.

Have you ever wondered how the image of a white Christ is received by other cultures? How do people in, say, Japan, Ghana, Guatemala, or India perceive Jesus? Actually, Jesus would have appeared as a Middle Eastern Jew: darker skin, black hair, and dark eyes. Itinerant preacher and healer that he was, it's doubtful that his garment would have been dazzling white. But we really know absolutely nothing of the physical appearance of Jesus. None of the gospel writers found it necessary to tell us anything about how he looked. You have probably read many biographies of famous figures in history that tell you something about their physical appearance, but nowhere will you find any words describing the physical appearance of Jesus. Why not?

Apparently, it was because an encounter with Jesus was about something else. How he looked didn't matter, because when you drew close to Jesus you knew him and recognized that you were standing in the presence of someone both out of and in this world. Being in his presence put all your assumptions into question, and you somehow knew that you were in the presence of a reality that transcended everything you held to be true, in favor of another truth about yourself and your life.

So, what was the nature of this presence? Would you have felt a certain power of love and acceptance that you had never felt from anyone before? Would it have been a kind of empathy that knew your hurts and sorrows in a way that no one else had ever known? Would it have been someone who understood the pain you could not quite put into words? Pain that you had never been able to share with another? Would you have experienced a power surging in your veins and muscles, a power that broke the lethargy of your life and made you stand tall, willing to give away your possessions — even your life — for a cause that seemed of ultimate importance?

Any or all of these may describe the presence people felt when they encountered Jesus. But for the crowd who met him in the synagogue that Sabbath day, it was something else that grabbed them, shook them, and astonished them about the man who was standing so near to them. It was his immediate and personal authority. This was an authority they had never seen before. But his only power was in his words. He had no force to back up his authority — except love. He spoke and acted as one who knew from whence he had come and where he was going, and he knew this with an unshakeable conviction that not even a cross could shatter.

In his gospel, Mark tells us what was so compelling about his authority was this: He invited people to live, not according to the laws and opinions of the scribes, but according to his compassion and God's truthfulness. People looked at him and listened to him as he spoke with authority about human experience. And they felt something that, for the first time, lifted the cataracts blinding their eyes and hearts to reveal a vision of living and dying that was God's truth.

Jesus spoke and people heard God! It was that simple, that beautiful, that enchanting, and that comforting.

You may think, in asking you to ponder what it might have been like to encounter Jesus, I have been spinning you a tale of long ago and far away. I have not been offering you a piece of historical biography. No, I want you to know that this same Jesus, who spoke with such immediacy and authority, is alive now. He is with you now. This same Jesus who spoke God's truth and astonished his listeners in the synagogue on a Sabbath over two thousand years ago is here, speaking with the gentleness, confidence, and conviction about the truthfulness of God.

Do you dare to open your heart to his presence? If you do, you will hear him speak to you of a forgiveness and a love so grand that it could take the soul of a dying thief into paradise. If you open your heart to his presence, you will hear a voice promising to walk with you in your journey through life and on into eternity. You will know his comfort when you encounter the turbulence of suffering and grief that you had thought would destroy you. You will hear one speak with authority who will lay upon you incredible expectations because he already knows what you have yet to discover: that you have been created in his Father's image and you have the potential, with his grace, to live a free, compassionate, and abundant life.

~~~

May you be blessed
to see what God sees:
the beauty and goodness
that dwell within you.

Harsh Realities

In my liturgical tradition, three scripture passages and a psalm are read during each Sunday worship service. I recall struggling to prepare my sermon during the season of Lent many years ago, when each of those passages was filled with doom and gloom, even horror. Each one seemed worse than the one preceding it. Jeremiah spoke of innocent blood being shed. Saint Paul spoke of enemies of the cross and those whose god is the belly and their base appetites. Jesus deplored the stoning and abuse of God's prophets. All three scripture passages are jarring, with their angry words. They remind the listener of something none of us wants to be reminded of: something is profoundly askew in God's creation.

If I were an angry preacher, full of bombast and predisposed to preaching hellfire and damnation, those three passages would have been a convenient way for me to unload. But I am not, by nature, an angry man, and I had a difficult time coming to terms with those seemingly offensive passages of scripture. I didn't particularly want to hear, or receive into myself, the message that something is deeply amiss in my world or myself. If I'm honest, I also didn't want to hear that I need to amend my ways.

Perhaps there is a blessing there, however, if we can listen through those words to what God is trying to say to us from the bottom of his endless heart.

"Blessed are the offensive, for they shall proclaim the kingdom of God," is not a beatitude you will find in either the Gospel of Luke or the Gospel of Matthew. Nor is it likely that this phrase will catch on and be plastered all over bumper stickers and wall posters. Yet it seems to encompass just what those Lenten passages point to. No one likes offensive people. They are big mouths who always say exactly what they please, no matter how tactless it might be. They act as if they are always right and know what everyone else should be doing with their lives. Offensive people are not concerned with social niceties and seldom find themselves acceptable in polite company.

Those scripture passages I mentioned are full of offensive people: the prophet Jeremiah, the itinerant preacher Paul, and the prophetic

Jesus, each one caught up, to the depths of their being, by a vision they won't let go. And they do not hesitate to open their mouths and say exactly what they think, no matter whom they might offend. The urgency of God's will is too great to be impeded by social niceties or accommodation to the world's agenda. Life is out of sync with God's purpose, and it is destroying all that could be good.

So Jesus has set his face squarely toward Jerusalem, to speak God's peace, no matter how offensive that might seem to be. Nothing will deter him. He even brushes aside a friendly gesture from some religious folks, a few Pharisees, who remind him how offensive he has become. They warn him that, for his well-being, it might be better to get out of town.

What is so offensive about God's peace, and why does this bring Jesus to the brink of losing his life? Was it because he associated with sinners and lepers and the poor? Because he dared to come down on the side of the dispossessed of society—the welfare cheats; the mentally ill, for whom no one speaks; the poor, for whom there will never be a job, other than standing in endless lines? Was it because he comforted the poor, confronted the rich, criticized the holy, and told them to love their enemies as much as God loves them? People who get caught within this vision of God simply do not fit into the world as it is. They have the audacity to take on the powers that be, as Jesus did with Herod when he called him a fox. This is what happens when God's will seeks to break into human life and transform it. Indeed, Jesus does offend a world that has lost its way in its own selfishness and has become immune to human suffering.

But that particular passage of scripture that shows the apparent wrath of Jesus doesn't end there. Look! As he stands there on the hill overlooking Jerusalem, you see that he is weeping. His heart is torn with compassion. Now it becomes clear that these are not words of anger that Jesus speaks. They are words of profound kindness. Jesus dares to come to us— we who have lost our way and whose lives are skewed and run amuck in our brokenness. God is not angry with us. He does not seek to offend us. He wants to befriend us with the deepest kind of friendship we will ever know.

Jesus uses an image of profoundest compassion to express what this friendship looks like. As he looks at Jerusalem (looks at us) he says, "How often would I have gathered you and your children together, as a hen gathers her precious chicks under her wings." Here is God's image of friendship that frees you to amend your ways. Despite your failings, despite your weaknesses, God gathers you into his arms to assure you, not of his anger, but of his everlasting love and forgiveness, like a mother hen who would take you under her wings to protect you. All he asks of you is a willingness to accept his love and forgiveness, a willingness to change and to share with him his loving compassion for those who suffer in his world.

Perhaps you have heard of a film called *The Elephant Man*. The film told the story of Joseph Carey Merrick. He was an English man with very severe face and body deformities who lived in the 1800s. This sad, disfigured man was first exhibited at a freak show in London before being sent on a tour throughout Europe. It was said of him that his appearance was so horrible and offensive that people fainted at the sight of his face, so that he had to wear a mask. One day a very lovely singer came to town and asked to see Mr. Merrick. The meeting was arranged, and they had a pleasant conversation. Just before she left, she kissed his ugly face. It was the first time anyone had loved him as he was, and tears trickled down his face.

All of us, deep inside, are elephant people. We yearn to be loved and accepted as we are. We lose our ways in life. We muck up creation. We hurt others. We ignore suffering. We become ugly to ourselves. To be reminded of that is what made the prophets so offensive to us. Can you hear, beneath their words, God's words of love for you?

God comes to you in profound compassion for your life. He seeks to take you under his wings and love you. He yearns to strengthen you so that you can dare to become his friend, in common cause with all you meet on your life's journey who are poor or suffering or hurt.

This friendship may offend. It may put you at odds with the world. But God's peace and love have always done so.

~~~

May you have the courage
of one unafraid
to allow the Gentle Healer
into your darkest places,
to restore you to wholeness.

Into the Desert

I invite you to accompany me on a journey to a strange place. I have a hunch we may discover something there. This is not the kind of place you would choose for a vacation and probably not the kind of place you would choose in order to find some respite from the daily stresses of living. There are no palm trees where we are going. No smooth, silky beaches or gentle cooling trade winds. Where we are going is not a place of rest. It is a place for struggle. A place to find the truth—perhaps the deepest truth in life we could ever discover.

So, come. Let us step out into the desert with Jesus, and let us somehow seek to experience something of what he encountered, according to what we know from the Gospel of Matthew. But let me warn you, before we enter the desert, that there is great danger there. A demon waits for us, ready to undo us. Here we go.

As we make our way into this strange place, let us simply ask questions along the way. Let us ponder what happened to Jesus when he dared to step into the desert alone. And let us also notice whether something in this desert could touch the deepest yearnings of our hearts, so that we can commune with the divine and be enabled to behold the eternal in the midst of all the noise, brokenness and fragmentations of our lives.

As we enter the desert today, I remind you that there were a number of early Christians in the 4th and 5th centuries—they are called Desert Mothers and Fathers—who chose to live out here in the solitude of the desert. They believed that the desert had been created as supremely valuable in the eyes of God precisely because it had no value for humans. The wasteland was the land that could never be wasted by humans because it offered them nothing. There was nothing here to attract hoards of vacationers, condominium builders, or shopping mall contractors. Those Desert Fathers and Mothers knew that here one could be alone with God, with nothing to do, nothing to create or produce. The desert is simply not a place to do anything; one can just *be* in the desert, alone with oneself or with another.

God seems to have had a love affair with the desert. It has always been a special place where he has led his people and where they would come searching for him: Moses on Sinai, Elijah at Horeb, Jesus in the Judean Desert that we now call the Mount of Temptation. These quiet places in the desert solitude are where God could be alone with someone, revealing the fullness of himself. The desert was the place in which the chosen and beloved people of God wandered for forty years, cared for by God alone. They could have reached their promised land in a few weeks, at most, if they had followed a map directly to it. But God's plan was to teach them that there was nothing they could do to secure themselves or produce valuable lives by themselves. God wanted them to learn to love him in the desert. He wanted them to look back upon their time in the desert as an idyllic time of their lives, when they were with him alone.

Now this is a very shocking notion, if you have really heard it. There are places and times in your life in which God invites you to discover and experience a new reality that has nothing to do with making and creating, with being active and busy and involved. In fact, there are times and places that God himself cherishes, when he can give himself to you when you have no other place to turn, no other source of strength. These are places of grace, the places of the gift freely given, when, for a few brief moments or hours, your whole life suddenly melts into the eternal and you taste the incredible goodness and beauty of God's presence and purpose.

Perhaps life has worn you down. Perhaps the burdens of your life — responsibilities, disappointments, illness, deep grief — have left you feeling empty, with few reserves left to help you cope. Perhaps you have wearied yourself in seeking your own renewal. Remember that God sends his own beloved son out into the desert to be renewed by nothing more than solitude, silence, prayer and fasting. Could it be that God is inviting you to do likewise? If you venture into the desert of solitude and silence, all that is required of you is to wait, listening for the inner voice of God.

We do live such frantic and compulsive lives. We are distracted by many things. Our culture places no value on doing nothing, but God seems to find this the one place where he is able to enter your life. Perhaps it will help to remember that Jesus's period of preparation for his intense ministry and for his depth of living is inaugurated by doing nothing except waiting, praying, and communing with the divine in silence.

In our fast-paced way of life, we tend to have an obsession for instant religion. We demand quick solutions for the bafflements of our journey through life. But, my friend, the spiritual life takes time and requires a lot of waiting. Sometimes we cannot hear God until we have spent much time in stillness, calming our restless and hyperactive souls.

Now we have been out here in the desert solitude with Jesus for nearly forty days. Here we are, you and I, and we haven't heard a sound for over a month, except the sand shifting under our shoes and the wind caressing our faces. We have spoken to no one, except ourselves. We have heard no voice except our own. Our souls are now as empty as our stomachs. Our roles, our titles, even our names have been stripped away. Waiting. Nothing happening. And then— suddenly—the inner voice speaks, and for the first time we grasp in three visions what has been hounding us and destroying us back in the city: food, security, power. The demon inside who tempts and tests us now has been inside us all along. But now we see, here in the desert where no life can be supported, that God comes to us with his manna, the sweetness of his presence. And we know we are depending on him alone, not our silly and anxious selves. For the first time, we love God alone as the creature loves the creator, and nothing less than this feeling of wholeness, beauty, and pure love will ever satisfy us in life. If we remain absolutely still, we may come to the awesome awareness that we are surrounded by angelic hosts and that we, like our Lord, can return to living in the city, renewed and strengthened to face whatever is before us, even death, for our Lord has shown us the way in the desert.

~~~

Come.
Lay down your worries and your pain,
lay down your fears and your
broken relationships.
In silence and in solitude,
be still.
Listen.

Down by the Riverside

*D*id you hear? There's a meeting, down by the river. Crowds are gathering and you can feel the expectancy in the air. Hopes are running high for new beginnings. Can you sense the yearnings? To be cleansed of the old, washed free from the past, groomed and fresh for something new. You can feel its uplifting power, so you hurry to the river, too.

But, oh! What a sight meets your eyes. Grown adults splashing around in muddy water like little children in the backyard pool. Someone dunked here, another dunked there, and here comes yet another wave of people tiptoeing into the cold water. And doesn't everyone look a bit silly as they emerge from the river, their clothes dripping wet?

Silly indeed. Outlandish and crazy to the uninformed observer who has yet to learn just how much the human heart desires to be cleansed. What has brought this crowd down to the riverside? I suspect it is the same thing that brings you to your knees, to your silent times with God, or to church. Perhaps you, like these in the crowds, are looking for something that you have not yet found. Is there something deep inside you that you would like to be rid of? Something that is making you feel bad, soiled? Something that is filling you with loneliness, even despair?

They came down to the river, their very souls trembling. They dared to hope for insight, self-recognition, and a glimpse of the real life they had ached for. They carried in their sacks all their disappointments. Their broken promises. Their betrayals. Their deaths. Their griefs. Their pain. The disappointments of those whom they had loved but who had not loved them. Their quarrels, their boredom and endless routines. Their emptiness and unbelief. They — like you — brought their humanity to the river, hoping for relief.

They also brought with them a deep sense of *ought* about their lives. What they ought to have done. What they ought to have been. And they were profoundly aware of what they were not. The words hung on their lips: "We have failed."

Even in our therapeutic age, when we try to rationalize away all the great oughts, or blame others when we fail, there still lingers within us that thin hint that somehow we have failed. Somehow we have sinned. We have not shared our plenty, even when we have been asked to do so. We have profited at the expense of others. We are prone to anger, quietly violent. Oh, yes, we do need to be cleansed.

Yes, you and I need to go to that river, too. We need to join that crowd. There is someone else in that crowd. His identity is hidden. He doesn't stand out; he melts into that crowd of humanity. He is like one of them, waiting to step into the river. He is like one of us. He lives among us, eats with us, drinks with us. He would be judged a sinner and would die on a cross between two condemned criminals. Down in the muddied waters of the Jordan River, his whole life is acted out that day as he stands in the water with sinners, even you and me. He doesn't mind brushing shoulders with such folks because his heart aches for them. His heart aches for us.

Yet clearly Jesus was different. He alone fulfilled the great oughts of life. He loved God. Again and again, in prayer, he bent his life to God's perfect will. He loved neighbors, as commanded, and he died for neighbors on a cross. No wonder the air was crackling that day.

No wonder we were all electrified when a voice spoke: "This is my beloved son. In him I am well pleased."

My hunch is that Jesus treasured those words and that moment through the remaining few years of his life. That love, that affirmation, that support, and that hope carried him through the darkest moments of his engagement with human reality. This is what buoyed him up, gave him his zest for life, and his relentless love for the dispossessed of life. And these words held him fast, even down to his last moment on the cross: "This is my beloved son. In him I am well pleased."

When you and I were taken down to the river (or to the baptismal font), often as tiny infants, we were baptized into this very baptism of Christ. As he became one of us, we have been made one with him. You who are soiled have been cleansed. You who have failed have been forgiven. You who have been searching have found a love that loves you as you cannot seem to love yourself. You who have despaired have grounds for the wildest of dreams. In him you are pure. In him you are holy. In him you are new, and you can face the future with hope and confidence. In him you are embraced, as you make your way through life, because, in him and through him, you have heard spoken to you: You are my beloved child, and in you I am well pleased. I am delighted to call you my own.

~~~

May you recall,
beloved child,
the freshening water of your baptism.
With you God is well pleased.

The Voice of God

Have you ever heard God speak? Hmmm. That's an uncomfortable question, isn't it? Are you squirming a little in your chair? Perhaps you think you *should* have heard God speak, but, well, you really haven't. What would happen to you, right this moment, if God suddenly began speaking to you?

There is a gospel story about two Greeks who approached Phillip...who then hightailed it to Andrew...who rushed to Jesus with their message: "Sir, we wish to see Jesus." Maybe you have that same yearning: Sir, we wish to hear God.

Are you hurting? Are you looking for arms strong enough to hold you in their love? Are you searching for peace deep within you? Are you sitting in darkness, seeking a glimmer of hope? If you whispered "yes" to any of those questions, then I think you are yearning to hear God speak.

The thing is, sometimes it is hard to hear God when he does speak. It's not that we need hearing aids or lessons in listening skills. I suspect that, deep down inside, we don't expect that God is going to speak. Or we have a confused understanding of God's spokesman—Jesus. Perhaps, never having heard God speak, we have simply given up expecting that he will.

The Nazarene stood there in the midst of a crowd, his knees beginning to shake. He had the ominous sense that his thirty-three years were suddenly beginning to telescope into a week. Time was slowing down. Something was going to happen in just a few short days or hours. Something was going to be accomplished through his life that few could ever dream of.

And the more he talked, the harder it became to hear him because there was tension in the air. You could hear his voice crack at times, like when someone becomes anxious. He starts talking about something glorious that is about to happen, but it makes so little sense when he jumbles it all up with grains of wheat falling into the ground to die and yield fruit. And then he pushes his words out—right at you and me—saying, "Whoever loves his life will destroy it." And it gets awfully hard for me to hear what he is saying, because I know I love life and I don't want to destroy it. And I have been struggling all my life to understand what he means when he says to me, "Lou, if you try to save your life, you will destroy it."

And it becomes even more difficult to listen to the Nazarene standing there—our Lord— admitting that his heart is in turmoil with fear and confusion. And he asks the question for all of us: Shall I say, Father, save me from this hour? Preserve my life, for God's sake! And then he catches himself. The Nazarene. Our Lord. And he utters: No, it was for this very reason, this purpose, that I have come to this hour in my life. The Nazarene stands there and says: Life has a purpose beyond mere survival. His life. Your life. Your life has a purpose beyond mere survival.

The air that afternoon in Jerusalem, the air that surrounded the Nazarene, was electrifying. And suddenly something strange happened in the midst of the gathered crowd. The voice of the Old Glorifier—the one who made the heavens and the Earth, the one who moves the stars and planets on their way—shattered the silence with his speech: *I will glorify your life. I will glorify every life that becomes your life.*

But the crowd that was there heard it and said, "It has thundered." Others said that an angel had spoken to the Nazarene. They had not heard the speech of God, because they had not expected that the voice of God would speak to them that afternoon.

Why could they not hear the voice of God? You and I know the answer already, if we have the courage to admit it. It was what the Nazarene, our Lord, was saying that cuts to the human heart: If you would preserve your life, you will destroy it. It is hard to hear that, even when the name of the one who is speaking to us is Love, for me and for you. Jesus is saying that life is more than survival of self. It has a purpose, an incredible purpose, if we can surrender ourselves to this love that sustains all that is.

For many of us, mere survival is our default mode. We awaken each morning planning our busy lives, and we collapse onto our beds at night recounting to ourselves all that we have accomplished. Or failed to accomplish. We worry about paying our bills, our less-than-perfect health. We worry about our children. Or our parents. Or both. We worry about job security. We waste precious hours comparing ourselves to others. Is it any wonder that we are exhausted?

The Nazarene's whole ministry is the voice of God speaking to us. Nudging us, persuading us, loving us into seeing that life is more than mere survival. Life is a road to glory when we surrender ourselves to the route whose direction is marked with the sign of the cross.

I cannot tell you in detail what your purpose is or how God's purpose for your life grasps you. But I can caution you that the culture within which we live is a culture that is satisfied to call God's speech only thunder or the rumor of angels. In our culture, to surrender means to admit defeat. But I do know that the voice of love that shattered the silence that dusty afternoon so many centuries ago continues to speak: This is the road to glory. Hear the Nazarene and live.

Not many of us know much about where we are going, really, with this life of ours. Not in the long run, anyway, except beyond the next mountain. We keep busy. We climb. We learn. We grow. But we are going, I believe, much, much farther than we can possibly see, and in everything we do, or fail to do, much more is at stake. In this life, and whatever awaits us, he is the way. That is our faith. And the way he is, the Nazarene, is the way of taking enough time to love our little piece of time without forgetting that we also live beyond time. It is the way of forgetting about ourselves and hearing the lives that touch our lives. It is the way of keeping silence, from time to time, before the power and grace that surround us and hold us in this strange world. It is the way of love.

Did you hear that? Was it thunder? Was it an angel? Whose voice was it? Will you surrender yourself to him?

~~~

May you love your little piece of time,
may you hear the lives that touch yours,
and in your silent moments
may you be held in grace.

What Amazing Grace Looks Like

One of my divinity school professors, a professor of homiletics (preaching) once admonished us: "No preacher should ever dare stand in a pulpit and think, or even hope, that she or he can add anything to this verse from scripture: For God so loved the world, that he gave his only child, that whoever believes in him should not perish, but have life, beginning now and stretching into eternity."

You are probably well acquainted with this verse—John 3:16. It is one of the most beloved verses in the Bible. I cannot remember ever officiating at a wedding in which this verse was not included. Somehow this verse summarizes everything the Christian faith has to proclaim. It is so familiar to us, though, that it has been worn smooth, like the pebble in the stream. And because this verse is so familiar, we may not hear the awesome words that bring us a truth that we could never manage to dream, even on our best night of dreaming.

For God so loved the world, that he gave his only child...

I invite you to open your heart, become vulnerable, and ponder these words in a fresh, new way. Try to absorb them into yourself. Allow these words to become what nourishes and sustains you, like the blood pulsing through your body and keeping you alive.

For God so loved the world, that he gave his only child. Yes, I did change the word from *son* to *child*. If you are a parent, you may find this wrenching. What kind of decision-making was going on one night in heaven? The night that God decided to give up his only child. I could never do what God did. I could not give up any one of my children for someone else. I would rather give up myself than give up one of my children. And you would, too. But the Scriptures do say, and we aren't very good at hearing it, God so loved the world that he gave up *his only child*.

And it says *he so loved*. Loved. How often have we used that word to describe something we feel? But how do we understand love in this context? What sort of strange love is this that is so vast that it can give up the only child, give the child up for likes of you or me? No marriage has ever known that kind of love. No friendship has known that affection. No child or parent has known that kind of love. A love that, one night, decided to yield its treasure for such a humble creature as you or me.

And it says that God *so* loved the world. And isn't there a difference between saying, "God loved the world" and "God *so* loved the world?" That one tiny word carries with it the passion of eternity. For us.

And it says that God so loved the *world*. The world and everything in it that God has made: every creature, every human being, every mountain and sea, every tree and flower, every cricket and centipede and seashell and lover that walks upon his beaches. God loves it all with such an incredible passion. And if God loves this world with such passion, then it must be a marvelous world. And ought we not cherish such a world and all that is in it, if this world is so precious to God? If God loves life with such a passion and even weeps for it and suffers for it, ought we not rejoice in it and cherish it?

For God so loved the world, that he *gave* his only child. He gave. He did not order or command his child. Nor did he sign a contract or strike a *quid pro quo* bargain. He gave a gift. But that gift has a hook in it.

If you're like me, you are not looking for a handout. You do not want something for nothing. It threatens your self esteem. Your self-reliance. And to accept a gift from another would be to bind you closer to the giver than you would like to be bound to anybody. And then there is this: if another human being dies on your behalf so that you can live, from that point on you can no longer live just for yourself. You also must somehow live for him. It's as if, in some sense, he lives through you now and, in another sense, you live through him.

If what he would do with his life is going to be done, then I have got to do it. My debt to him is so great that the only way I can approach paying it is by living a life as brave and beautiful as his death.

So maybe I would have prevented God's child from dying if I could have, but since it is too late for that, I can—and you can—only live life for what it truly is. Not a life that is mine by natural right, to live any way I choose, but a life that is mine only because he gave it to me. And I have got to live it in a way that he also would have chosen.

Go outside some clear, star-filled night. What do you see? The romantic sees the star light, star bright, first star I see tonight, wish I may, wish I might, have the wish I wish tonight. The scientist sees balls of gases hurtling through space at the rim of the universe, millions of light years away. I look to the stars, or into the eyes of another, and see the love that moves the heavens and planets on their way. A love so vast and mysterious, and yet so humble and gentle, that it surrenders his only child in death on a cross, that I may know life. The name of that mysterious love, in front of which all fear melts, is God. Or amazing grace, if you will.

~~~

May you have the courage
to live your life
as bravely and as beautifully
as the One who gave his life
in love
for you.

The Power of Wounded Healing

We live in a world of scientific reality in which all of life is the subject of investigation, in order to figure out how it works. If you have figured out how life works, then you can control it and, presumably, fix it. So healing has become the province of the expert. Healers in ages past learned the healing properties of plants, herbs, and roots. Today the healer is usually the physician who has an armament of machines, drugs, scalpels, or surgical procedures. We give thanks to God for these gifts of medical wisdom and technology, the most marvelous gifts humanity has ever received. But, unfortunately, we have become among those who believe that this is all that healing is. And if that is so, then we have lost sight of the reality that healing — true healing as the Bible understands it — is more than removing illness. Rather, true healing is nothing less than salvation.

John the Baptist languished in prison. He sent several of his disciples to ask Jesus if he was the one whom God's people had been expecting for generation after generation. The one who would finally break the stranglehold of sin and evil in human life. Or would humanity have to continue its painful waiting?

In response to his cousin's question, Jesus replies: Go tell John what you see and hear. Go tell John about the credentials of my ministry, the infallible signs that God is present, in his fullness: "The blind see again, the lame walk, lepers are cleansed, the deaf hear, the Good News is proclaimed to the poor...and blessed is the person who does not lose faith in me."

Jesus does not point to church programs as a sign of God's nearness. He does not point to money raised for his cause. He points not to the numbers who joined his army (which, incidentally, were very few). No, he points to the healing of suffering as the infallible sign of God's kingdom, and he says that he is doing the work of God's kingdom. If we were bold enough to recover the essence of our own ministries, it would look like this: "He called the twelve together and gave them power and authority over all evil spirits and to cure disease, and he sent them out to proclaim the Kingdom of God and to heal." (Luke 9:1)

What is it today that is in need of healing? In some cases, it is our bodies, but in most cases it is our souls that are afflicted and diseased. No era in history seems more uncomfortable with death and illness, despite all the technology. No era of humanity is as preoccupied with the individual—meeting the needs and desires of the individual or proclaiming the rights of the individual. No age has seen the degree of social and family disintegration as has our age. Consequently, we are tempted to judge and blame and harshly criticize those of our country or community who cannot make it on their own: the ill, the anxious, the handicapped, or the poor. Yet these are Jesus's people, and their healing is the infallible sign that God is in his world.

Perhaps you and I are strong and healthy and not in need of healing. But might there be, hidden behind our apparent strengths, a myriad of weaknesses? Hidden behind our proud hearts and seeming self assurance are deep doubts about our goodness, our worth, our value. Hidden behind our apparent faith is deep doubt about the goodness of life, another name for which is despair.

The Bible tells us that these are the kinds of people—people like you and I—who have no other place to turn for healing and wholeness.

The Bible tells of all the people who have been driven to life's limits. People who, down deep in their hearts, sense that nothing short of the salvation of God can heal their brokenness. Jesus called them the humble, the meek of the earth, the pure in heart, and the poor in spirit. They were those for whom the only treasure in life was the salvation of God and the calming of their bodies and souls with a peace that cannot be obtained through this world. Can you be honest enough, in your human condition, to turn to Jesus for healing?

How is it that Jesus heals? Why have the sick always come to Jesus for healing? Because he manifests a life of infectious healing power. That is why we are told, again and again throughout his ministry, "...and he healed their sick and cast out demons from their souls." Even sick people who only came near him or merely touched the hem of his garment were healed. But, you ask, in what way does Jesus actually heal the sick person? Is it through some magical power? It sometimes looks like that, but Jesus repeatedly says, "Your faith has made you whole." These are not magical healings. Healing is never magic. These are healings brought about by faith. And who is it in whom you will have faith or trust? It is one who has known you from your birth, shared life with you, known what you have experienced, and known what you suffer.

In what does the healing power of Jesus's life consist? What was, specifically, his power to heal? It is this:

> That evening they brought to him many who were possessed by demons; and he cast out the spirits with a word, and healed all the sick. That was to fulfill what was spoken by the prophet Isaiah, "He took our infirmities and bore our diseases." (Matthew 8:17)

So Jesus's power to heal is found in his power to suffer. He does not heal by eliminating disease and abolishing it, but by taking our sicknesses upon himself. People are not healed by Jesus's supernatural powers. They are healed through his wounds. Jesus takes our sufferings in life upon himself as his wounds, and he heals them by sharing his life and his hope with us. No matter what we suffer, even death, Jesus has shared it. He has been wounded by it and has offered it up to God to be healed. God heals all our sorrows and accepts all our tears by taking them into himself and making them his own pain. Our God is willing to suffer to make us whole. And that is, ultimately, the meaning of love.

Can you grasp this awesome way of God? Can you bear witness, in our age of science and technology, to God's healing power? If you can, then do you dare to follow the way of Jesus, to be open and vulnerable to the wounds of others by receiving their wounds into yourself? Henri Nouwen describes such people as wounded healers, and our Lord has empowered you to become one of them.

~~~

Healer of our every ill,
light of each tomorrow,
give us peace beyond our fear,
and hope beyond our sorrow.

-Marty Haugen (1957—)

Shaped by the Potter

Have you ever tried to throw a pot? It's not as easy as it sounds. Now I'm not talking about taking that dried out old geranium up onto the balcony and heaving it into the woods. No, "throwing a pot" is the jargon used by those who make pottery. It's what a potter does when she takes a lump of clay and places it on a spinning wheel to mold and shape it into a form before it is placed into a kiln.

Unless we know what it is like to throw a pot—the real subtleties and fine art of this task—we are not going to be able to grasp what the prophet Isaiah was saying when he says, "You are the potter, oh Lord, and we are the clay." Anyone in Israel would have known immediately the incredible power of this image. It wasn't until my wife took a pottery class that I could appreciate what Isaiah was really saying when he acknowledged God as a potter and his people as lumps of clay.

I am sure that your image of the potter working with a piece of clay suggests to you that what is important is giving the clay a shape.

Without the potter's careful touch upon the clay, as it spins upon the wheel, it comes out formless and shapeless. But there is something far more important that precedes shaping the clay, and if you don't get this right, everything else is hopeless. The most important thing for the potter in throwing the pot is getting the clay centered on the wheel. If you don't get that lump of clay centered, then, as the wheel spins, the clay will either collapse or go flying off the wheel. You see, the clay has no power in itself to center itself. But if it is not centered, it is worthless. No creation is possible...only chaos and formlessness.

I am sure you can begin to see now where Isaiah was going with this ancient image when he suggested that the Lord is the potter and we are the clay. Unless life is centered in the potter who creates, then not only is it misshapen, but it collapses or goes flying off in all directions. We are at loose ends, so to speak. There is no shape or beauty to our lives. Our lives are fragmented. Our pots won't hold water.

I invite you to become centered in this culture that seems to spin dizzily, without direction, without shape, and often without purpose. I do understand how very busy you may be. How pulled in so many different directions. Is not this the very time, then, to pause and turn inward toward a God who would center your life? A God who would shape it and give it real form and beauty?

So how does one go about this sort of centering? Even to admit the validity of this image is a radical first step. To see your life and your being as clay. But then, many folks get off track because they believe that they are the ones to shape their own clay. So, to get that one thing straight—to fully believe that it is God who centers your life—is a profound second step. But look again at that clay. It is silent. It awaits the loving hands of the artist to fashion it, to center it, and make it beautiful and valuable. So perhaps the next step is waiting patiently, entering into silence, knowing that you are not just sitting there, like a lump of clay, but that you are making yourself ready for the potter. This potter, in God's good time, will take up the wheel and begin the spin. He will begin to hold you in his hands, shape you, and make you into something beautiful.

In a word, this process means waiting for grace, knowing that you will be shaped. Knowing, ultimately, that you cannot shape yourself, lest the kiln of life fire you into a piece of brittle and useless rock.

And the potter will remake you in his image, and this image will be revealed as one who is Christ-like. Are you ready to be fired in the kiln of God's purifying grace into a stunning vessel of his love?

~~~

May stillness and grace
enter into you
while you patiently await
the gentle molding of the potter.

Do You Dare?

Any fisherman worth his salt knows that the best catch is just when darkness begins to ebb, before the first rays of sunlight. That's when the fish swarm. Now the morning sun had already warmed the air, and a Galilean breeze stirred the water. They were sitting in the boat together, James and John and their father, Zebedee, a few feet from the shore. The knuckles of their hands ached from tying knots in their frayed nets. They had already put in a long day, even though it was still morning, and their bodies were sore. Oh, but they were weary. Bone weary. Heart weary. Life weary.

Their father had taught them all they knew about casting nets, mending nets, and setting prices, but he was aging rapidly. He could hardly throw a net anymore, but he came along each morning because it was the family business. He wanted to help, but clearly his sons managed the catch. Simple survival bound these generations together as tightly as the knots they tied in their nets.

Three men approached the beach, edging toward the anchored boat. Suddenly, without introduction or greeting, the silent mending of two generations was torn apart. A voice called out, "Follow me!" Immediately they left the boat and their father, and followed him. (Matt 4:22) And Dad watched as his sons dropped their mending, waded to the shore, and vanished from his sight. And his heart cracked as he sat there, staring in disbelief at the empty shore.

This was not the first time these haunting words had invaded hearts and changed lives. Simon and Andrew had also given one last heave to the net, straining to snatch the last possible catch before the sun rose too high. It wasn't a bad way to make a living, casting those nets. There was some security. People always had to eat. Not bad for people who could neither read nor write. The man had approached them in the morning sun and, without any introduction, his words reached out and grabbed their hearts: Follow me! Immediately, without hesitation, they dropped their nets. Which means they dropped their lives on that beach—to follow a dream.

What kind of power stood behind those simple words, that some should abandon their families, others their secure jobs? Is it really the case that when God gets in your blood he wrestles with you about what seems most dear—your relationships and your vocation? Sometimes when God is in your blood, it even changes who you are, as Simon found out when his most precious possession—his name—was changed to Peter, the rock.

Do you really want to follow him when your vocation is at stake? Your family in question? Or even your name—your good name? What got into the heads or hearts of these fishermen that morning on the beach in Galilee? Is that any way to make an important decision—to drop it all right there on the sand? Walk away from your father? Stroll away from your livelihood and endanger your pension, as well as your social security?

What is so confounding in all this is that what we hold valuable—our rationality, our calculations, our perceptions of how we make important decisions—are all thrown to the Galilean wind. People in their right minds do not act this way unless they have gotten out of their minds and something has gotten into their hearts.

It is striking that this whole scene turns on the word *immediately*. First the words, "Follow me," and then the response—immediately. Command and response. Both are immediate because this is a pregnant moment when something profoundly new is going to be born. Immediacy is in that Galilean air because those two words are about to shatter a worldview. And when that happens, you can do one of two things. You can stand there and think about it, or you can give your heart away and chase after it...another name for which is faith.

Have you also heard these same words, spoken by the same voice who uttered them to Peter, Andrew, James, and John on that Galilean beach? Is that voice beckoning you, in the silence of your heart? And what do you do with the immediacy of these words, once you have heard them...really heard them? Perhaps you are a bit like me—plain scared! Or maybe like Father Zebedee. Why didn't he get up out of that boat and hurl his aging body behind the Christ? Is it our maturity that causes us to hesitate? Our skepticism that compels us to remain seated in the boat? I'm too old for this kind of thing. Or too wise. Then come the questions and the doubts.

Why should I follow? How far should I follow? Where do I follow? How much can I take along with me? What will I get for all my pain and sacrifice? What will it cost me? And as I sit in the boat with Father Zebedee, the rest have disappeared over the horizon.

Then there are the questions that are really only one question: who is this who speaks such stunning and frightening words? You need to know who he is before you drop your net and throw your life to the Galilean winds. And that is understandable enough. Except that the grand paradox is this: it is only by first following him that you begin to find out who he is.

Have you begun to perceive the awesome dimensions of what it means to live in faith? To follow him? And once you have heard the words, you cannot help but decide whether to sit in the boat or step out into the unknown with nothing — absolutely nothing— to guide you but a hand just beyond your grasp.

For most people, stepping out of the boat and into the unknown will mean staying right where you are, but in a totally new way. It might mean letting go of your family, in order to have them back in a new way. It might mean the sudden awareness, in your job or your studies, that God is trying to transform your world. Have you been shattered by loss, illness, or grief? God may be trying to heal your broken life.

Where will you end up if you step out of the boat, leave your nets, and troop after Jesus? Who knows? Some say it all ends up on a cross. Others say that he lives. You will never know unless you throw it all to the Galilean winds.

Are you still sitting there?

~~~

When the voice beckons,
enfolding your weary life
with sweetness,
and when your little boat
suddenly feels too small,
may you be brave enough
to step out
in faith.

Listening to Angels

*P*eople today enjoy being entertained by science fiction. Darth Vader and Luke Skywalker are locked in mortal combat. Worlds swirling through the cosmos await the triumph of one of those celestial warriors. *Star Wars* was born with this science fiction fantasy. Mr. Spock turned his celestial ship from years of reruns on TV to the movie sets. And there was indeed life out there that came to meet us here in *Close Encounters of the Third Kind*. Close encounters of an intimate kind. No more intimate, however, was the encounter with that loveable creature from outer space: E.T. The celestial doll and friend of children whose task it was to jerk our tears and remind us that invading beings from the celestial sphere aren't that bad after all, and that love, somehow, traveling the speed of light, can traverse the universe.

Is science fiction just entertainment, from which the movie companies and producers make big bucks? Or is there something else, just beyond this earth-bound life of ours, that reaches out beyond itself? Do we not yearn so deeply to hear that there is something out there that is so awesome in its power that it can triumph over what seems to be the persistent evil in this world? We want so desperately to believe that there is something more. Something more fulfilling than what we struggle with or trudge through each day. Wouldn't it be nice to hear that the last word—*the last word spoken about our own personal life*—is a good word we can count on?

Are E. T. and his relatives the best we can do for angels these days? Perhaps we see them as angels of the modern day—fantasy reminders that there is far more happening in the universe than rising at 7:00, heading to work at 8:00, collapsing in fatigue at 5:00, and trudging off to bed at 11:00. At some time, not too long ago, did we make a bad bargain? When we traded our religious hope for the future in favor of the life promised by the progress of science or politics, did we also trade away Michael, Gabriel, and all the angels?

My friend, I do not think there is a single soul who doesn't harbor the hope, if not the belief, that there is life—many forms of life—pulsating beyond the Milky Way. Yet take the same poll about angels, and few will get beyond the arguments of the Middle Ages about the number of angels that might dance on the head of a pin. We will entertain the notion of celestial aliens of other worlds in the universe, but angels? Oh, today they're pretty much reserved for ornaments on Christmas Trees.

Whatever happened to angels? St. Michael and his army of heavenly hosts? Is it a bit bold (or maybe rather quaint) in these sophisticated times to even talk about angels? Yes, it is bold — and we need to do it! Here's why. Angels are messengers. The very word means just that: a messenger. Angels bear the message and the promises of the holy beyond us. They are God's messengers. Their existence itself is a message: that there is a word to be spoken, a message to be uttered throughout the universe. Even to the hidden corners of your heart. It is the *final word*, uttered from beyond all the sorrows and the brokenness of this life. It is God's word. God's utterance that he has triumphed. You and I have triumphed. This life is open-ended.

In the prophetic Book of Daniel, St. Michael and all his angels wage war in heaven (Did you catch that? There was even war in heaven!), at the very foot of God's throne. And God's messenger bears God's final word of life's victory into eternity.

Maybe only children can hear the message, because children can let their minds wander into the truths of science fiction. Children can laugh and play with E. T. But if you can trust in the angels as God's messengers of hope, if you can trust God's triumph in the wars in heaven through the blood of the Lamb, then perhaps you and I could laugh more and perhaps be a bit more playful with life. Beyond all the seriousness of life, beyond the sorrow and the heartache, God awaits, speaking the last word. His is the final word of peace and hope, richness and goodness in this life and in the life to come. If we could trust God's final word, would we not take ourselves a bit less seriously? And, most importantly, would we not love more? Share more? Care more, as angels ourselves who have a message to announce to others?

Jesus caught a moment of divine insight. He took his disciples aside and spoke of God's triumph. They had been out and about, healing the sick and casting out demons, and had just come home to the Lord, bursting with enthusiasm and joy at their success — particularly their power. They were like children who couldn't wait to tell Mom or Dad the neat thing that they had discovered.

They blurted out, "Lord, it's unbelievable! We have power in your name! Even the spirits are subdued. The technology of our healing is awesome, Lord!" Like children of our century, they were awed, impressed, and excited by their power to control and demonstrate success.

And Jesus said to them: "Don't rejoice in this, that the spirits are subject to you, but rejoice that your names are written in heaven." *Our* names are written in heaven. Our names are written into the history of God. That is our destiny. That is our source of joy. That is why we are not frightened, or bereft of hope, or at the end of our rope. And angels will come to speak to us, if we will listen, while scribes record our destiny in God's life.

~~~

May angels enfold you
with their heavenly assurance
that your name is written in heaven.
May this knowing accompany you
each day of your life.

Where Are You?

*T*he silence of the garden is shattered by a deeply probing, deeply searing voice, like a parent searching for a child hidden somewhere and trembling with fear. The voice cries out its haunting question: Where are you?

God is searching, seeking like a parent who has lost a child. He is seeking his creature. Adam was God's first creature to hear that haunting question in the garden, and he shrank back in shame and fear as the questioner neared his crouching body.

Although Adam was the first to hear the question, "Where are you?" you, too, have probably heard that same question in the depth of your heart. Not in the primitive garden, but deep in those moments when you are alone with yourself, in those private times and spaces that you share with no one. This is the place where, when you scan the wide horizon of your life, you already sense that you are lost. That's when the question seeps into your awareness: Where are you? And you know that it is someone else asking the question, and you sense the painful rightness of the question, because you know that in your journey through life you have, indeed, lost your way. Something has been broken. Deeply shattered. And you cannot put it back together again.

This story from the Book of Genesis, many centuries old, is an incredible moment of insight into the human condition. You don't have to wait for Freud or Jung or a counselor to reveal the nature of the condition in which you find yourself. The ancient book tells us that we have shared in a common experience, a deep sense that something is fundamentally amiss in us that requires healing. It is something that requires salvation.

This story from Genesis, told again and again, is so familiar to us, perhaps because we can see ourselves in its characters. The story is a masterpiece of brevity, crafted with great poetic skill, as the three characters, God, Adam, and Eve, interact. Listen to them, and hear the ancient insight into reality.

God, the loving father, comes searching for his beloved child, asking, "Where are you?" It takes one Hebrew word to ask that direct and straightforward question. But listen now to the answer: "I heard the sound of you in the garden, and I was afraid, because I was naked; and I hid myself." It takes seven long Hebrew words to answer God's simple question. Seven long words of explanation and rationalization. And what could not be hidden or concealed in the words is the fact that four times the pronoun *I* stands out in bold relief. The ancient book thrusts out before us, in a most poetic way, the fundamental issue in human existence: the centeredness in self. Defensively, self-defensively, caught in the snare of his own self, Adam reveals the fracturing of humanity into self-centered personhood.

But it doesn't stop there. The trial continues. God inquires, "Did you eat of the tree I commanded you not to eat?" Did you overstep the limits of the life I gave you? Now listen to the reply: "The woman you gave to be with me, she gave me the fruit of the tree and I ate." We may have heard this story so many times, that we fail to grasp the astonishing response of casting blame, projecting, and disowning responsibility. A flat-out refusal to take responsibility for one's own behavior. When Adam blames the woman—it was her fault, not my fault—suddenly the most intimate of human relationships is rent asunder, and henceforth no human relationship will be free of this fissure. The once harmonious relationship between people has now become the grounds for pain and brokenness. In the words of the hymn by Scott Hyslop, "In Adam We Have All Been One."

It was bad enough that he betrayed a human relationship to justify himself, but Adam goes on justifying: "It was the companion that *you, God,* gave me." So now he is blaming God for the whole mess in Eden. And in just a few sentences, the storyteller has brought into stunning clarity the fundamental issue of Adam's "I" now standing in judgment upon God. This is the ultimate act of disobedience because it is the assertion of self as the divine center of realty. Not only are human relationships shattered, but so is the fundamental relationship between God and humans.

This is not a popular interpretation to make today in a culture willing to rationalize away much of human behavior or responsibility, but the ancient book suggests that what has shattered life in all its relationships is disobedience. In other words, transgressing the limits of freedom. And few of us want to acknowledge that our freedom may have limits.

You know, Eve doesn't come off all that badly. At least she doesn't betray her companion, nor does she blame God. Instead, she implicates nature. "It was the serpent…and I ate," she quickly admits. But she weds herself to Adam with the "I," and there they stand, bound together in their self-centeredness, a wedding of belligerent egos. Why did she do it? I have heard a lot of bad reasons, but the one that rings most true to me is that she doubted what she had heard. It was Adam who told her God's truth, so she had heard it second-hand. It isn't curiosity, but, rather, the seeds of doubt that undermine life.

So here we are, on the other side of Eden, you and I, and in Adam we have all been one. It is a grim but honest picture that Genesis has painted. But the story does not end there. There is a beautiful moment of grace in this story from Eden. God looks down upon the man and the woman, wed together in their brokenness, shame, and vulnerability. It is a pathetic sight, the two of them standing there in shriveling fig leaves, garments of their own hurried making. So God, like a loving mother, takes a needle and thread and, with the compassion of a parent, stitches clothes of skins to warm and protect these beloved creatures. This God who asked, "Where are you?" is a God of compassion.

And the story won't end there for any of us who have all been one in Adam and Eve. God seems to have a love affair with gardens. He transforms life in gardens, from Eden to Gethsemane. He will reveal, in his beloved child, the depth of obedience, and in the tomb in a garden he will refashion life anew. It is the story of salvation, from garden to garden, from brokenness to healing, from enmity to the possibility of living together as precious children of our loving parent. A steadfast love unites this whole great story from garden to garden, saving us from ourselves and empowering us to live beautiful, redeemed lives.

~~~

When danger lurks
in the garden of your life,
may you know the One
who nurtures and cares for you
like the most loving parent.

A Word of Grace

Sometimes the grace of God can be overwhelming and far beyond our capacity to comprehend or grasp. The grace of God can seem not to fit very well into our worldview because our worldview is something we have fabricated. So sometimes the grace of God can be shattering. And sometimes it has to be, to break through and be heard. And yet, for those who can hear and for those who can bear to have their world turned upside down, the grace of God can be so overwhelmingly beautiful, so healing and restorative.

Here is a strange setting for an encounter with the grace of God: a house in a village where thirteen men are huddled together after a long day's journey. (But aren't all journeys are long — especially the one we call Life?) Oh, they are so weary. Their bodies ache and they yearn for rest. No heavy conversation, just a bite of food to assuage their grumbling stomachs and a place to lay their heads for sleep.

And then the Rabbi asks, "What were you discussing on the way?" The twelve are stunned. Tense. How does he know? Is he psychic? The silence is thick, heavy, and almost oppressive. Have they been caught? Caught in the act?

Remember when you were a child and did something wrong? Remember how your mother asked you the question that betrayed to you that she knew exactly what you had done? The silence of the twelve was the silence of shame. No one spoke, and only Mark can tell us what they could not say: On the way, they had been discussing with each other who was the greatest. It is almost comical, if it weren't so tragic. Grown men snooting about with one another, arguing about who amongst them was Number One. Never mind that they were all unknown entities who couldn't read or write. And isn't it rather tragic that the greatest among them had just told them that he was about to die for them? You and I can laugh or weep at them but, mind you, we were both walking down that road and later huddled in that room.

I know that I am guilty of what those disciples did—and I'll bet you are, too: measuring yourself against someone else. Of course, it's not something you and I do in public, but it is right there in our inner dialogue, and it reflects the depths of our personal insecurity. Some people are honest enough to admit their judgementalism, others far less so, but everyone is guilty of this. In fact, it may be our chief preoccupation.

And because this measuring, this judgementalism was the chief preoccupation of the disciples that dusty day, they could neither hear nor understand the words of grace when Jesus spoke them. In his Epistle, James suggests that the consequences of such inner measuring are devastating. It is the sort of thing that can destroy human relationships, ravage life, and oppress other human beings. Where inner measuring is waged, there can be no room for compassion, James says, only death.

But Jesus was patient. One wonders how he could be patient with such silliness that was so dangerous. But thank goodness he is, because he has to deal with the likes of you and me. So he sat down with the twelve again and said: Look, folks, here is the way it is. If anyone would be first among you, he must be last of all and a servant of all. And with those words he turned their world — and our world — upside down. He shattered those false worlds with words of grace.

Jesus must have seen the puzzled and skeptical looks on the faces of the twelve, so he took a little child and put the child right there in the midst of these grown men whose inner insecurity had driven them to argue about who was the greatest. And then he puts his arms around this child, and it seems almost cute and romantic. But this is grace, in all its beauty, shattering worlds to speak the truth. And Jesus says: If you can accept this little one who has no value in your world, and if you can be this child's servant, then you are among the first, and in so doing you have received God himself.

It is a moment of grace if you have heard — really heard — what Jesus has offered you, because it is true liberation from the constant inner struggle to be someone, in comparison to someone else. For once, you are free from yourself because you belong to someone else. And you don't have to prove anything.

In one gracious move Jesus has revealed a new way to live. Really, it is the only way to live because the other way is so destructive. Call it servanthood. Those who have mastered servanthood are those who have come to be called the greatest, and they have known a freedom from the anxieties about life that gnaw

at the heart. Can you hear that? Really hear it?
And if you have heard it, will you dare to live it?

~~~

May you be released
from the urgent striving and comparing
that wearies your very soul.
And may you dwell in the grace
that offers you servanthood.

A Blessing for Uncertain Times

You had thought the course would be straight.
Well, mostly straight.
The way ahead looked clear. And, besides,
you had companions with whom to share the
journey.

You did not anticipate — could not have
known — there would be so many boulders on
the path.
You never thought the blue skies would crackle
into angry grey.
And where are those companions now?
The wind has become cold, and you wrap your
arms around yourself
and pull your thin coat closer.

But, most of all,
you never expected to feel so lost, this far into
your journey.
Never thought the familiar would look so alien.

This blessing comes to you through the
boulders, the angry sky and the cold wind.

It cannot vanquish them, but it can take you to a safe space.

This blessing reminds you to stay awake. Alert. It reminds you that even when the way is unfamiliar, there can be surprises. A small fawn in the thicket. A tiny flower beside the path.

A bit of bread.
A sip of wine.

This blessing will stay with you until you find your way.
And the thing about this blessing is this.
It is sticky.
It will not leave you.

A Final Word of Comfort

*T*here are few words in all four Gospels more comforting than these: *Do not be afraid, little flock, for it is your Father's good pleasure to give you the kingdom.* (Luke 12:32) Whenever I read these words or sing the beautiful and simple hymn that is based upon them, I feel consoled. Comforted. My anxious mind and troubled heart are eased by the powerful promise of God's pleasure in giving me the kingdom and the fullness of life that implies.

But no sooner have we taken our ease in those reassuring words, than we are shocked and baffled by what Jesus says in the very next verse. He utters this jarring imperative: Sell all your belongings and give the money to the poor. Provide for yourselves purses that don't wear out, for they will be your treasure in heaven, where no thief comes near and no moth destroys. For where your treasure is, there your heart will be also.

Suddenly the gift and the Father's good pleasure seem to have a string attached. Or a rope. Or even a chain. What are we to do with these embarrassing words of Jesus, "Sell all you have, and give the money to the poor?" Really? Not even his church has ever truly taken those words at face value. What do you do when you come up against those words of Jesus that simply don't fit into your world? Can you selectively omit them? Ignore them? What would a Biblical literalist do with what Jesus advised? I have never met one who has taken these words of Jesus literally.

One thing is clear. Jesus could not have intended this to be a platform or a program to provide for the poor, because surely he knew that hardly anyone would take him seriously on a matter as grave as this. No one is going to have a yard sale for all her belongs. Nor is he going to put everything he owns into trust with the Salvation Army.

So what are we—you and I—going to do with these words? Jesus did speak them, and we cannot ignore them, especially when they were spoken by someone who practiced what he preached.

Perhaps we can look for guidance at a few of the heroes of the Hebrew Bible, Abraham and Sarah. Abraham and Sarah were two old folks who found themselves one night in a sweet tangle of love, conceiving a child, when most folks their age were shuffling around a nursing home pushing their walkers. God was faithful to his promise, and his two servants were faithful to his promise.

They were searchers. Seekers. Dreamers who were somehow never quite at home in this world. Call them homeless people, if you like. Home was somewhere else, lying way out there in the future. And so they wandered through the landscape of life believing promises and chasing dreams. They looked beyond every sweet thing of the world, waiting for God and craning their necks to glimpse the fulfillment of a promise. And there were others, like Moses and the great King David. What distinguished these people is that they saw themselves as strangers and nomads on earth. Because they never made the mistake of believing that they had found their home in this world, they could do what so many of us, deep in our hearts, would like to do.

The Bible remembers these people and holds them up because each one carried a light suitcase to eternity. Their suitcases were not chock full of possessions. They did not travel in caravans of U-Hauls. Tents were all that covered their heads at night. And they were strangers on earth.

Such an unusual way of looking at life seems to be pleasing to God. The author of the Book of Hebrews says: *That is why God is not ashamed to be called their God.* Even though each one of them was really a scoundrel in his or her own way, God was proud of them and quite pleased to be associated with them in their poverty of spirit and poverty of life. And not one of them, according to the Bible, was ever disappointed by faithfully chasing after God and his unearthly, pie-in-the-sky promises.

And it was just that—being faithful, trusting beyond trust, believing beyond belief, dreaming beyond the wildest dreams, and behaving at times in the most god-awfully peculiar ways—that somehow led God to reckon each one of them as his kind of people. People with whom he wants to spend eternity.

That's the way it was with Jesus and his dreaming about a kingdom or a reign of God in this world, the likes of which few would ever see, but all would seek and search for with all their might. Because the God of Abraham, Sarah, Moses, and David had promised that things would someday be changed for those who kept hoping and believing.

Maybe that was something of what Jesus had in mind that day when he uncorked these words upon his disciples. He wanted them to get beyond all the appearances and to get at the life of trusting and chasing a promise down the road and all the way into the kingdom. Because that was the real stuff, and still is the real stuff, of life. Is the phrase, "Carrying a light suitcase into eternity," really a softening of what Jesus said? Perhaps it is, but I find it helpful.

I also find it helpful to ponder that maybe comfort—real comfort—is actually something quite different from what we conceive it to be, or what we yearn for it to be. Maybe it means hanging on blindly, empty-handedly—to promises. Hanging on in faith for what we cannot see, but has been whispered to us. Hanging on in faith, trusting, and believing. And perhaps comfort is best pronounced *challenge*. To be comforted is to be challenged to one's limits.

Honestly, I do not know what to do with Jesus's words. I can only take them into my heart and ponder them and bravely open myself to be challenged to the core of my soul. May you do likewise, fellow dreamer.

CPSIA information can be obtained
at www.ICGtesting.com
Printed in the USA
FSHW020833260521
81724FS